the 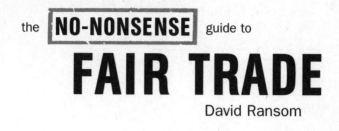 **NO-NONSENSE** guide to

FAIR TRADE

David Ransom

The No-Nonsense Guide to Fair Trade
First published in the UK by
New Internationalist Publications Ltd
Oxford OX4 1BW, UK
www.newint.org

in association with

Verso
6 Meard Street
London
W1F 0EG
www.versobooks.com

Cover photo: The Stock Market

Design by Andrew Kokotka/Ian Nixon, New Internationalist Publications Ltd.
Production editor: Troth Wells

Printed by TJ International Ltd, Padstow, Cornwall, UK.

British Library Cataloguing in Publication Data.
A catalogue record for this book is available from the British Library.

Library of Congress Cataloguing-in-Publication Data.
A catalogue record for this book is available from the Library of Congress.

ISBN - 1 85984 334 4

the **NO-NONSENSE** guide to
FAIR TRADE
David Ransom

Foreword

'IS THERE ANY "bottom line" other than price or profit?' asks David Ransom in this timely *No-Nonsense Guide to Fair Trade*. It isn't a new question – John Ruskin debated the same thing at length over a century ago – but it has become one of the central issues of our new century. It is so much more central than it was, because trade is so important and because business is now so widespread and such a powerful force in the world.

When I started out in business, the model in my head was provided by my mother's café. Working there taught me that business wasn't about financial science. First and foremost, it was all about trading – about buying and selling – and about a different kind of bottom line, which meant that you could bring your heart to work. You didn't have to leave morality safely at home to work there. Nor did you have to leave behind the understanding, sympathy, humanity or fun that is essential for business, just as it is essential for life.

It was a lesson I've never forgotten. As I see it, my mother's café also embodied a much newer model of business that seems to be emerging, though slowly and with enormous difficulty. Unfortunately, most of the planet suffers under the yoke of a slash-and-burn style of trade that understands none of these things – what David Ransom calls 'unfair free trade'. What in the 19th century was about the freedom of communities to trade equally with each other has become a license for the big, the powerful and the rich to ride roughshod over people who have no choice about whether they trade or not.

When business can roam from country to country with few restrictions in its search for the lowest wages, the loosest environmental regulations, the most docile and desperate workers, the destruction of livelihoods, cultures and environments can be terrifying. It's the survival of the economically fittest, they say. But the interpretation of 'fit' by so-called 'free' traders – the marketable, the profitable, the global – is pathetically inadequate. It's a kind of fascism, just as fascism was a perversion of Darwin's survival theories.

The financially 'fit' survive. Those that don't fit – people, communities and nations – are bled dry. It's a devastating machine that can bear no variation, and it will not build the kind of world most of us want.

This isn't a battle between community or money – it's between a bottom line that includes communities, ethics, families and the environment, and one that sees nothing but money. And I know which side I'm on.

That's why at the Body Shop we have been putting resources into building a different model of 'community trade' that can point a better way forward. Our emphasis is now on supporting smallscale economic initiatives wherever we go, keeping communities vital. Anything from supporting black family farms in America – almost an endangered species – to building a new fiber economy, supporting new ecological designers or teaching our employees community organizing.

It's a model that puts partnership at the heart of trade. Take, for example, our project in Tamale in northern Ghana, where we have been sourcing shea butter from a cooperative made up of women from 13 villages. Trade has changed the status of women in these communities. Because they now have a livelihood, they can pay for books and uniforms for their children. They can call on a health worker when they're ill or a midwife when they're pregnant. Young girls who would once have automatically been put out to work can now get an education and a sense of opportunity. By working together with this small trading cooperative, we have been able not just to change people's lives, but also to change the way people see the world.

But we have had to learn too. We have had to understand their culture and restrictions, what they are able to do and what is difficult for them. We have had to understand their passions and we have all of us changed as a result. Me included: community trade will change us all.

'There is no wealth but life,' wrote John Ruskin more than a century ago, and that's the real bottom line. If trade undermines life, narrows it or impoverishes it, then it can destroy the world. If it enhances life, then it can change the world.

That's why David Ransom's book is so urgent. It is a crucial part of the argument for trade with a different bottom line, and it's never been so important. That's why I'm delighted to commend it.

Anita Roddick OBE
Founder & Co-Chair, The Body Shop

the **NO-NONSENSE** guide to

FAIR TRADE

David Ransom

CONTENTS

the **NO-NONSENSE** guide to

FAIR TRADE

A whistle-stop tour through the short history of international trade and a few snapshots of the scenery. How 'free' trade and the law of comparative advantage came to rule the roost, and who's been paying for the consequences. What fair trade is trying to do about it.

AS IN LOVE and war, all's fair in trade. The very idea of 'fair' trade looks, from one point of view, to be at once a statement of the obvious and a contradiction in terms. It's obvious that you can only buy something from someone who wants to sell it, and vice versa – trade is a voluntary exchange between consenting adults and therefore fair by definition. Equally, 'fair' trade is a contradiction in terms because trading comes naturally to people and regulates itself through the self-righting mechanism of market forces. You can't buck the market. As with rain forests or the ocean tides, you meddle with trade at your peril. Morality simply doesn't come into it.

This orthodoxy has prevailed for a good while now and it might have a better claim to survive were it not so patently absurd. Who are these people who can't buck the market, a system they themselves invented, supposedly in their own best interests? What is the likeness between market and environmental forces, when the one conspires to destroy the other? Markets and trade are human constructs and therefore susceptible to human failings – not least in this respect, that by aspiring to infallibility they are less able to learn from their mistakes.

So what is fair in trade, who says so and why should we believe them? There is a simple test and you can obtain the results by asking two simple questions: who benefits and who is accountable? In the case of orthodox 'free' trade, the answer to the first question is straightforward: the already rich and powerful. It is, in other words, patently unfair. The answer to the second question is, if anything, even simpler: no-one. Unfair trade is the mortal enemy of democratic accountability, which gets in its way. Fair trade is primarily about reasserting human control over a mechanism that claims to be in the best interests of everyone but no longer even bothers to prove it.

History can tell us something about how we got into this fix. The word 'trade' has had a surprisingly short life in the English language but its meaning has changed all the same. Originally it described a path or track marked out by the passage of human feet. From the 14th century onwards it was also applied to the course of a ship. By extension, it came to suggest a way of life as well. A couple of hundred years ago (and sometimes even now) people were said to 'follow a trade' – the craft of a stonemason, tailor or carpenter, who stood somewhere between 'professional' and 'laborer' in the hierarchy of class. To one side of grand entrances to stately homes and smart hotels you can still sometimes find signs indicating 'Tradesmen's Entrance' round the back. Only in the 20th century did trade come to signify exclusively the exchange of things for profit. The process by which a way of life became a way of making money tells us most of what we need to know about the trouble with the word as it's currently understood.

The adjective 'free' creates other difficulties when attached to it, as routinely happens in orthodox economics. In the 19th century, industrial capitalism spread around the world through the muscular sinews of European empires. Most of them had been founded on military conquest and were maintained by brute force. They operated a variety of 'mercantilist' trading systems which prohibited commercial exchange with rival empires – or anyone else – without official approval and profit. The ultimate purpose of foreign trade was to enrich and glorify the rulers of the colonial power, whether that was Spain, Portugal, France, Britain or Holland.

Comparative advantage

As industrial capitalism grew in wealth and power, particularly in Britain, it was in need of a theory to justify why it, rather than assorted royalty and landed gentry, should be the legitimate heir to the riches that could be harvested from international trade. The theory of 'comparative advantage' was deployed early in the 19th century to explain why trade unencumbered by mercantilist restrictions would eventually be better for everyone – and, quite coincidentally of course, industrial capitalists too. Interminable, arcane disputes between free-traders and their rivals began and continue along remarkably similar lines to this day.

The notion of comparative advantage is usually attributed to the British millionaire stockbroker and entrepreneur David Ricardo. It was a refinement of the theory of 'absolute advantage' first devised by Adam Smith. According to this theory, every part of the world has an economic advantage of some sort. So, for example, Britain in the early 19th century had an advantage in the industrial manufacture of cloth. It had liberal supplies of coal, made the steam engines that powered the mills and, as people were forced off the land into industrial cities, plentiful labor to work them. The former British colony in America, on the other hand, had an abundance of agricultural land, a shortage of urban labor and, in the south, the right climate for growing cotton. So it made sense for

America to send cotton for manufacture into cloth in Britain and to buy cotton cloth from Britain in return. Both countries were better off this way, making the most of their advantage and the 'international division of labor', than they would have been if they had each tried to do exactly the same thing.

'Comparative advantage' complicated matters somewhat by suggesting that advantages operated within as well as between national economies. So, for example, although England produced both wheat and iron more cheaply than Poland, its comparative advantage in iron was greater than its absolute advantage in wheat. So it made sense for England to import wheat from Poland, even though its own wheat was produced more efficiently. Poles would be better off because it cost them less labor to buy English iron with their wheat than to produce iron themselves. The English would be better off because it would pay the Poles to offer sufficient wheat for English iron to make them net gainers too. In this way, international trade worked to maximize the efficiency of every national economy. Hard to prove, but in the right voice it could be made to sound pretty convincing.

Ricardo or Marcet?

The trouble with this proposition begins at the very beginning, for it was not David Ricardo who first came up with it. Mrs Jane Marcet was a prolific author of textbooks on topics as diverse as chemistry and philosophy and wrote imaginary 'conversations' between girl students and their teachers. A year before Ricardo published his *Principles of Political Economy, and Taxation*, Mrs Marcet's *Conversations on Political Economy* appeared with the more or less complete theory of comparative advantage set out in the form of a dialogue between 'Caroline' and 'Mrs B'. Needless to say, her achievement has gone largely unrecognized and the attribution to Ricardo remains. Economic orthodoxy is as susceptible to prevailing prejudice – in this case, the inferiority of women and the superiority of stockbrokers – as any other.

So, when it comes to comparing advantages, the view you take rather depends on where you stand. Aspiring US capitalists, for example, had good reason to appreciate the disadvantages of comparative advantage. More profit could be made from cotton cloth than from raw cotton. The process of industrial manufacture added 'value', which was reflected in the high price of the cloth relative to the raw cotton commodity. Americans could capture more of this value, in profits and employment, if the cotton mills were in America rather than Britain. Comparative advantage as it was interpreted in imperial Britain at the time would have kept American cotton producers comparatively poor while making British mill owners very much richer. American capitalists got upset about this sort of thing. It just wasn't fair. After all, they had put up much of the cash for the war of independence from Britain that would eventually launch the American capitalist juggernaut – and American cotton cloth, like denim – onto an unsuspecting world.

Slave labor

The cotton fields of the American south were, of course, run on slave labor. For hundreds of years the slave trade had operated much like any other, if a great deal more profitably than most. From the point of view of America's cotton barons, slavery must have looked like an advantage to beat all others – without it they'd have been out of business. The freedom to indulge in it was as stoutly advocated then as free trade is today. However, those budding industrial capitalists couldn't operate their new factories on slave labor. Slavery worked very profitably in rural, agricultural settings, but not in industrial, urban ones, where a wage-earning workforce could be hired and fired at will. Slavery undermined the 'free' market for labor – like any other commodity – that the industrial revolution required. That was one of the issues on which the American Civil War was fought and won – in good measure by the wealth of industrial capitalists once again.

The Great Depression

In other words, it is quite impossible to detach economic orthodoxy from the prevailing disposition of wealth, power and self-interest. The more you think about it, the more absurd becomes the notion that 'free' trade has ever existed – or ever will. The clearest indication of this comes from those regular occasions when capitalism goes into one of its slumps or depressions. The worst of these – so far – was the Great Depression of the 1930s, in the brief years between the two great wars, when the system itself seemed to be on the verge of collapse. Today's free-traders will tell you that what went wrong then was that governments tried to protect their national industries from the effects of depression by raising tariffs against foreign competitors, thereby stalling international trade and compounding the ruin. This interpretation has given 'protectionism' a bad name ever since.

Less partisan accounts, however, also notice parallels between the generally indolent stance of governments towards the internal workings of their national economies – and mass unemployment in particular – in the 1930s, and the inertia of national governments in the face of free-market 'globalization' today. Leastways, capitalism in America recovered in the 1940s only with the aid of lavish government spending on employment programs and the Second World War – scarcely a prime example of the self-righting mechanisms and benign effects of free-market forces.

After the experience of the 1930s and 1940s, a conscious effort was made to industrialize the newly independent colonies of Europe in Africa and Asia, as well as Latin America, in the 1950s and 1960s. That way, it was felt, nation-building could begin and international markets for industrial goods would expand much faster, to the benefit of everyone. In the South, government programs of 'import substitution' encouraged 'infant industries' to set themselves up, protected behind tariff barriers against foreign competition.

In some places, like Japan and the Little Tigers of Southeast Asia – notably Hong Kong, Singapore, Taiwan and South Korea – this worked pretty well. With their own new industries protected behind import barriers, these countries set out to be 'export-oriented' and produce things for world markets. In other places – particularly in Africa and Latin America – it worked pretty badly, creating inefficient industries that limped along, trying to supply local markets and consuming enormous subsidies, until they finally expired. Nonetheless, international trade and the world economy experienced its 'golden age' of growth without precedent, and without issue either.

Export-led growth

By the 1970s the failures of import-substitution were too obvious to ignore. When combined with the collapse of the Soviet Union after 1989, they gave the free-marketeers renewed determination and confidence. After all, even if the free market proved as disastrous as before, where was the rival, what was the alternative? A fashion for 'export-led' economic growth began to sweep the world, based on the success of the Little Tigers. The idea was that, since world trade tends to grow faster than individual economies, producing for 'world markets' is the most efficient and profitable way to go. Deregulation removed the very idea that governments could usefully intervene. The results have been very satisfactory indeed for the chief advocates of the experiment – banks and transnational corporations. For almost everyone else, and particularly since the crisis in the Little Tigers that exploded in 1997, they have been very much less obvious.

Many of the countries of the South remain today just as they have always been, entirely dependent on producing basic commodities like cotton for world markets. Their experience of world trade has been utterly disastrous, and for reasons that are not in dispute. There is no quicker way to make – or lose – a fortune than by

The origins of the World Trade Organization

As World War Two was coming to an end, a spirit of 'never again' briefly prevailed over international affairs. This led to the founding of the United Nations in 1945. The original intention was to create subsidiary agencies accountable to the UN, including the financial institutions that eventually became the World Bank and International Monetary Fund. There were plans for an International Trading Organization.

However, powerful business interests succeeded in separating the economic from the political institutions. A downgraded General Agreement on Tariffs and Trade (GATT), with just 23 of the West's richest countries – excluding the Soviet 'bloc' – was founded in 1948. Its purpose was to resolve trade disputes through a series of negotiating 'rounds', the last of which was launched at the up-market Uruguayan resort of Punta del Este in 1987.

One of the agreements eventually reached by the 'Uruguay Round' of GATT was that it should transform itself from an ad hoc agency into a proper institution, or World Trade Organization (WTO). Above all, GATT had no 'teeth' or formal means of enforcing its decisions. The collapse of the Soviet Union after 1989 created a large number of potential new members – though China remained problematic. Meanwhile, the advance of globalization opened up the prospect of a truly global agency enforcing free-market values with an armory of sanctions and fines.

The WTO was eventually set up in 1995 as the successor-body to GATT. From now on, trade negotiations would be conducted in the single currency of the market – the price in hard cash. 'Process' issues affecting the environment or human rights were specifically excluded. Although the great majority of the world's nations now belong to the WTO and in theory have an equal say, many cannot even afford to be represented, while a few of the most powerful routinely make decisions on their own. The first serious challenge to these values came at the Ministerial meeting of the WTO in Seattle in 1999, where – among other things – plans for a grand 'Millennium Round' of negotiations had to be put on hold. ■

speculating on international commodity markets. A frost kills the coffee harvest in Brazil; a war disrupts copper supplies from Zambia; a speculator attempts to 'corner' the silver market: all such events cause sharp fluctuations in prices and unequaled opportunities for profit – or loss. The effect is compounded by vast amounts of money switching in and out of commodity markets in London, New York or Chicago. Even larger sums of speculative money swill around the currencies in which world trade is transacted. So the soundest financial advice is always to avoid commodity markets like the plague – unless you can afford to lose your money. Today, the poorest countries least able to afford it are the most heavily reliant on world commodity markets for their very survival. This is about as close to economic insanity as it is possible to get, though economic orthodoxy wants them to get closer still.

Deep in debt

In good measure because of this, many such countries are now deeply in debt. So they have been forced by their rich creditors into 'structural adjustment' programs. These are a form of bankruptcy administration, modified only by the fact that you can't 'dissolve' a country or a people in quite the same way as you can a company or a corporation. Among other things, structural-adjustment policies require debtors to export whatever commodities they can lay their hands on in order to earn foreign currency with which to service their debts. Because every debtor is ordered to do this at the same time, there follows an entirely predictable glut of commodities on world markets – and prices plummet. Who is to say that this was not the point of the whole exercise?

The winners once again are speculators, banks and corporations, as well as everyone in the North who benefits from the low levels of inflation that cheap commodities from the South make possible. The losers are the world's environment – as precious nonrenewable resources are wrenched out and recklessly squandered – and poor people's redoubled impoverishment. So the free-trade balance looks very much less favorable when viewed from the South, which is where the majority of the world's people see it from. Some advantages on world markets are evidently more comparative than others.

International trade now, at the outset of the 21st century, looks very different from the way it did at the outset of the 20th century. The European empires have almost vanished. In their place is a single empire of footloose corporate capital, dominated by the United States.

Associated with this is a profound change: the majority of the world's manufacturing labor force has moved from the North to the cheap-labor countries of the South. In export-processing zones that run in a band around the most heavily populated regions of the world, from Mexico and Central America through the Philippines, Indonesia and China to India, Pakistan and Morocco, many millions of people live and work in conditions resembling most closely those of 19th-century Europe or America. As the hard labor of manufacturing has moved South, so a 'post-industrial', 'post-modern' or 'information' economy seems to have emerged in the North. In reality, things still have to be made, but power and wealth have slipped away from industrial labor into the hands of the corporate citadels and finance houses of the North. For the majority of the world's population in the South, the advent of the new century has been accompanied by a retreat into the conditions of an increasingly distant past.

Where the power lies

Then, as now, the most pressing issue for everyone caught up in the maelstrom was the absence of any notion that people should, or could, intervene at all in their shared destiny. Most of our democratic aspirations

The terms of trade

A key element of international trade is the 'terms' on which it takes place. Individual countries earn foreign currency from exports and spend it on imports. So, for example, one country might export rice and import oil. If the world price of rice halves, or the price of oil doubles, then it will have to export twice as much rice to import the same amount of oil. Its 'terms of trade' are then said to have worsened or become more 'adverse'.

The critical thing is not just the price of rice, but its price relative to everything else. This is the problem with exporting commodities such as coffee beans, or raw materials such as mineral ores. It's not just that the 'added value' of processing the coffee beans or turning the ores into metal is lost to the exporting country. Over the years, the world price of commodities has tended to fall relative to the world price of manufactured goods. So any country that exports largely the former and imports largely the latter is in trouble.

This is precisely what has overtaken the poorest countries in the world, particularly in Africa. Odd things then begin to happen. For example, a hungry country might find it's exporting more and more food grains because that's all it has and the world price has fallen – which means food gets scarcer at home and its price might actually increase for the hungry local population. Very often, imports considered 'essential' are of things like cars or electrical goods which benefit only the rich in poor countries. In this way, worsening terms of trade are felt in declining standards of living and increased poverty for the majority.

But it's not just 'physical' trade that matters. Commodity exports are used to pay rich countries for increasing foreign debts – so even more has to be exported, without increasing the wealth of poor countries at all. It's a downward spiral with no obvious way out. Taking from the poor to give to the rich is the only guiding principle involved. ∎

The terms of trade in Africa

Change
1997 1998
-0.2 -0.6

Impact on real incomes
1997 1998
-0.1 -0.3
-2.6 -2.4

-9.9 -9.1

All Africa

Sub-Saharan Africa

Human Development Report 1999, UNDP.

today are focused on national or local governments – most of the decisions that matter are taken by transnational corporate empires, backed by the United States.

These empires are the most active advocates of 'free' world trade simply because they monopolize two-thirds of it – a much greater share than they have of internal or 'domestic' trade – and want to keep it that way. They do not mean 'free' in the commonly understood sense of the word; merely that it should continue to operate in their interests.

Paradoxically, they rely very heavily indeed on governments to achieve this. They receive lavish cash handouts from the public purse: subsidies, bailouts (for banks in particular), tax breaks, 'incentives', hard currencies in which to do business, 'diplomatic' assistance and commercial espionage, publicly funded scientific research, government contracts, credit guarantees, 'policing' operations like the World Trade Organization (WTO), an educated, trained and compliant workforce, roads, ports, airports – more or less anything that takes their fancy. Such is the extent of public subsidy to private, corporate enterprise that it is they, rather than those who rely on meager welfare benefits, who truly deserve the title 'scroungers'. In return they fund political parties in rich countries, sponsor corrupt individuals in poor ones – which comes much cheaper, but amounts to the same thing – and gain a political stranglehold as well.

Controlling the beast

The question is not whether intervention in trade is necessary or desirable, but what kind of intervention there is to be; not whether trade should be 'regulated' or 'deregulated', but whether it is to be the servant or the master of people. Though the human interest in this matter may have only the faintest of voices at present, it is getting very much louder because the most urgent priorities for the majority of the world's people are so similar – and so blindingly obvious.

The first is inequality. A cornucopia of things may have been conjured into existence, but it is available only to a small and shrinking proportion of the world's people – at best, just 20 per cent. Because the wealth of unrestrained capitalism doesn't just exist, but accumulates, it makes the rich relatively richer, the poor relatively poorer and the gap between the two absolutely wider at an accelerating, compound rate. Democracy cannot conceivably survive, let alone flourish, within or between societies where such blatant injustice intensifies by the day.

The second concerns the nature of capitalist wealth itself. For example, everyone knows that global warming and climate change are already upon us and have to be stopped – or there will be an end to our children's children. Yet prevailing economic orthodoxy dictates that there is nothing much to be done.

The birth of fair trade

Just as well, then, that for the past 30 years or so a small but determined and growing band of pioneers has been working on the practicalities of trade done very differently. Can it be made to work for, rather than against, impoverished commodity producers in the South? Can the process of production be democratized, ownership shared, organized labor encouraged, child labor made unnecessary, environmental sustainability and human rights promoted? Can consumers be induced to think – and pay – more than they currently appear to believe is necessary? Is it possible to survive, even to prosper, both 'in and against' the conventional marketplace? Is there any 'bottom line' other than price and profit?

The idea of fair trade is not new. In its contemporary form it has developed in parallel with the process of globalization. From the 1970s onwards, aid agencies and their associates have been working with craftspeople in

Consuming passions

There's a scale of inequity that varies with different kinds of consumption. Basic necessities like food grains are consumed in a broadly equal fashion by the world's population. High-protein foodstuffs like fish or meat are less evenly distributed between rich and poor. Consumption of electricity, telephones and paper is progressively more concentrated in the hands of the rich. At the extreme, 90 per cent of all private motor cars are owned by the richest 20 per cent of the world's population. Four-fifths of total consumption expenditure is accounted for by just one-fifth of the world's population.

Measured in terms of environmental costs, rather than just money, the maldistribution is even more extreme because the rich consume much more of the things that cost the environment most, like fossil fuels and metals. We shall, of course, have exterminated ourselves entirely before the rates of car ownership in, say, the US are ever replicated across the world's population as a whole. That means dealing with the private motor car in the US and the North, rather than turning for salvation to the further impoverishment of the South.

Conventional notions of 'wealth' tend to create an autocracy of consumption. The contrast between rich and poor, equity and injustice, gets sharper the more 'advanced' the technology involved – the majority of the world's population has yet to speak on the telephone, for example. This is not an argument against technology, merely that its usefulness has no other measure than the well-being of humanity as a whole.

As a general principle, the closer wealth is to being consciously conceived and universally shared, the more 'sustainable' it is likely to be – and vice versa. Fair trade is also about the role world trade plays, for good or ill, in this process. ■

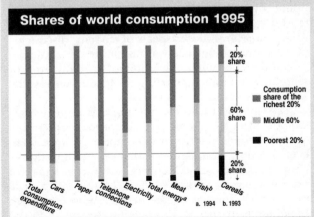

Human Development Report 1998, UNDP.

Shares of world consumption 1995

20% share
60% share
20% share

Consumption share of the richest 20%
Middle 60%
Poorest 20%

Total consumption expenditure · Cars · Paper · Telephone connections · Electricity · Total energy[a] · Meat · Fish[b] · Cereals

a. 1994 b. 1993

the South to satisfy a taste for 'ethnic' household goods and ornaments in the North. Alternative retail outlets were set up. Solidarity movements with places like Nicaragua began to make use of trade in traditional Southern commodities, such as coffee, to increase awareness and raise funds. More recently, fair trade has moved on to use conventional retail and marketing methods across a range of tropical food products, looking for a wider impact on the 'mainstream' through supermarkets and sophisticated advertising campaigns.

One way or another, unfair free trade is now on trial. That involves discovering exactly how and by whom the things we consume are made, and examining the evidence. Conventional trade relies on our remaining blind to this kind of evidence. The greatest single virtue of fair trade is that it encourages us to take a closer look, to engage more critically with the intriguing, sometimes shameful, details of everyday human life.

This *No-Nonsense Guide* considers fair trade in its wider sense, as the seed of an alternative that can flourish more vigorously than is sometimes assumed. Little attention has yet been paid to the subject by the theorists and researchers of the new world economic disorder – there are, for example, precious few books on fair trade. Meanwhile, and unlike some of the more grandiose aspects of current 'discourse', there is something practical that more or less any of us can do to promote fair trade in our daily lives, by searching out and supporting those alternatives that are already available.

It's tempting to dismiss the topic as impenetrably tedious. After all, people must adapt to overpowering 'global realities' and learn to compete on world markets or simply go under – so what's the point of quibbling? Common sense, however, suggests a degree of caution when we're presented too bluntly with a 'reality' to which 'there is no alternative'. Almost certainly, someone is trying to short-circuit reason, political debate and the alternatives. In this case at least one alternative is to follow more closely the path trade takes between our lives and to listen to the untidy human story that is told in the chapters that follow.

We begin by looking at one country, Mexico, at a critical time in its recent history, when it was on the verge of signing the North American Free Trade Agreement (NAFTA). Mexico is the only Southern country that borders directly on the US, so the issues here are in very sharp focus. We pay a brief visit to coffee producers in the southern state of Chiapas just before New Year's Day 1994 – an even more critical date here, since it marked the start of an uprising that made waves around the world and continues to this day.

In the second chapter we meet the *cafeteleros* – coffee farmers – of south-eastern Peru, at the start of the long and winding road the coffee bean follows to reach its international market. Along the way we encounter a recurrent theme – the impact of international trade on local environments, in this case on the valley of the great Tambopata River at the headwaters of the Amazon.

The cocoa trail

For the third chapter we move from Peru to Ghana, a country that relies on the export of cocoa beans for all sorts of basic necessities, including government revenues. Ghana is in the grip of a structural-adjustment program imposed by the International Monetary Fund (IMF) and World Bank. As it turns out, the results for the cocoa farmers, who were supposed to be among the winners, are ambiguous to say the least, though fair-trade cooperation makes a difference.

Bananas have lent their name to a variety of republics and wars. Chapter Four reports from the battlefield of the latest Banana War in Central America and the Caribbean. From the plantations of Guatemala and the small farms of Dominica (one of the Windward Islands) there are some unexpected lessons for the High Court of Globalization, otherwise known as the WTO. Not least of these is the way it has, in effect, been promoting slave labor and environmental insanity. Lost in the fog of war, you wouldn't really expect to discover a perfect, fairly traded, organic banana – unless, that is, you chanced upon it in the Dominican Republic.

With the shift of manufacturing labor from North to South there's plenty of territory beyond the traditional trade in commodities for fair trade to invade. Blue jeans are something of an icon for consumer capitalism and 'The American Way', but the consequences of the trade that makes them are pernicious and reach round the world. Chapter Five suggests that consumer capitalism, replete as it is with fashionable labels, can't actually deliver on the promise it makes of

The measure of fairness

It would be easy for fair-traders in the North to get carried away by the need to agree and enforce common standards. However, they have to take great care. Unless Southern producers are involved in the process from the start, then fair trade simply replicates the consumers' control over producers in another form.

There are two main 'umbrella' groups to which most fair-trade organizations around the world now belong. Fair Trade Labeling Organizations International (FLO) is based in Bonn, Germany, and brings together a growing number of fair-trade labels. For some time it has been developing closer links with producers.

The International Federation for Alternative Trade (IFAT) is a global network of 145 fair-trade organizations, many of them producers, in 47 countries. It is controlled by its membership.

FLO and IFAT have different functions and therefore slightly different standards – not all of their members necessarily observe them all, and neither FLO nor IFAT has direct power over their membership, though peer-group pressure has considerable influence.

These are some common principles of fair trade:
● *Democratic organization* – producers must be able to exercise control, by owning the land on which they work, by being organized into cooperative or democratic associations or in other ways appropriate to particular settings.

unlimited choice, even between pairs of blue jeans.

In Chapter Six, we catch up with the cocoa beans from Ghana again as they find their way around corporate Big Chocolate in Britain. Under the watchful eye of Koto Asamoah Serebour, some of them also get into fair trade – and a much better deal for farmers like him. For the time being, far too much still depends on the strange and manipulated tastes of the consumer, but here at least there are some excellent alternatives on offer.

Fair trade – the way forward

The episodes of this story have been gathered together from accounts first published in the *New Internationalist* magazine over the past decade or so, but not previously compiled into a single volume. The ones about cocoa are the work of my colleague in

● *Recognized trade unions* – where ownership is vested in others, then workers producing for fair trade must have the right to organize and negotiate through free trade unions.

● *No child labor* – though child labor is a much more complex issue than is sometimes suggested, its use is incompatible with fair trade.

● *Decent working conditions* – the above measures help to create good working conditions and pay, but there is a need to ensure them in any event.

● *Environmental sustainability* – fair trade is becoming increasingly 'green', in part because prices for greener products (like organic food) are generally better, but primarily because producers themselves prefer it.

● *Price that covers the cost of production* – this usually means providing a minimum-price guarantee, regardless of world commodity prices.

● *Social premiums to improve conditions* – fair trade is a different kind of transaction, and so in many cases a premium is paid that doesn't go directly to individual producers but to their organizations for collective projects.

● *Long-term relationships* – that extend beyond specific contracts to purchase and may involve a much longer-term commitment if mutually-agreed conditions are met. This matters both to producers (so that they can have some certainty for the future) and to fair-trade purchasers, so that supplies are available even in the rare 'boom' years when prices are high and the need for fair trade seems less pressing. ■

Toronto, Richard Swift. The rest are the author's though subsequent events have made some updating necessary. For the most part, much less has changed than would have been both possible and desirable.

The point is to restore to trade its essential purpose – either it enhances human well-being as a whole or it is a worthless enterprise that enriches some, impoverishes many more and gets us all precisely nowhere. The commitments made to each other across vast distances by fair-traders invariably offend in some way against the law of comparative advantage and so are potentially subversive. For current economic orthodoxy to prevail, and for the horizons of what is conceivable to remain so meanly restricted, all that is required is for the alternatives to be made to seem irrelevant. The stories that follow show just what nonsense this really is.

1 Mexico: a cautionary tale

How international trade affects a whole country. What the North American Free Trade Agreement (NAFTA) was supposed to do for the only Southern country that borders on the United States – and what actually happened. How coffee farmers in Chiapas can tell the difference between 'free' and fair trade.

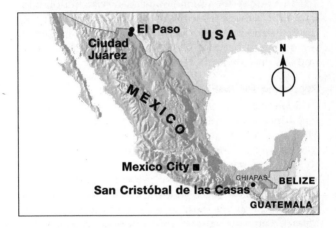

THE AVERAGE MEXICAN is neither desperately poor nor disgustingly rich. That, at any rate, is what the conventional economic measure of 'Gross National Product per capita' in Mexico tells you – what the place looks like if you average out its wealth across the population as a whole. The trouble is that wealth in Mexico is not averaged out equally across the population. Mexico has the fourth-largest number of dollar billionaires in the world – the 35 richest families control as much wealth between them as its 15 million poorest citizens. That, rather than the average, is what makes Mexico characteristic of the world as a whole.

Unfair international trade transfers wealth from relatively poor countries to relatively rich ones. But, increasingly, it also transfers wealth between rich and poor people within individual countries. Governments of all kinds – local, regional or national; democratic or otherwise – are told that they cannot act to restore some measure of equity or environmental sanity without distorting the rules of free trade, placing themselves beyond the pale of market forces and the 'international community'.

Fair trade is not a niche that can survive in isolation. It cannot get very far without confronting current economic orthodoxy. If it begins to work then it does so not so much because it's a good idea, but because it impacts directly on poverty and inequality.

Preparing for NAFTA

In September of 1993 I went to Mexico to research a magazine about the country. The Governments of Mexico, the US and Canada were putting the final touches to the North American Free Trade Agreement (NAFTA). It was due to come into effect on 1 January 1994, bringing down most of the remaining trade barriers between the three countries, ostensibly to the benefit of all of them. With its huge pool of cheap labor, Mexico's enviable comparative advantage in labor costs would surely now be able to take full effect, and some very rich Mexicans expected to get even richer.

The official mood in the country was euphoric. The Mexican Government had outspent every other lobbyist in Washington to see NAFTA through the US Congress, and had clearly begun to believe its own publicity. Mexico was about to defy the geographical imperative, kick the dust of its desert frontier with the US from its shoes and join the North, where it rightfully belonged. At the Mexico City headquarters of the PRI (the Institutional Revolutionary Party), which had ruled the country since 1929, spokeswoman Roberta Lajous explained to me just how ambitious her plans were. 'If I could move the whole of Mexico to Europe

I would,' she said. 'In fact, it would fit rather neatly into the Mediterranean Sea.' The aphorism that Mexico is eternally 'so far from God, so close to the United States' was about to lose its sting.

Skeptics there were, to be sure. The economist Ifigenia Martínez of the Party of Democratic Revolution (PRD) told me: 'It will prove impossible to continue with this rotten system. It is constructed to serve the interests of very, very few people, and it simply cannot continue.' But then, presidential elections were in the offing and that was the sort of thing you had to say if yours was the thankless, occasionally dangerous task of breaking the political stranglehold of a regime that had survived longer than any other in the world.

Even so, it was hard to square the PRI gloss with what I had already seen in Ciudad Juárez. This is the Mexican half of a sprawling desert city that straddles the border with the US and becomes El Paso, Texas, on the other side of the Rio Grande. Ciudad Juárez has mushroomed around its export-processing *maquiladoras* – the cheap-labor, export-only assembly sheds run by big-brand corporations that were the focus of all those official hopes for a bright future in Mexico City. I managed, with some difficulty and the help of a local collective of prostitutes, to get into a *maquila* making television sets for the giant Dutch electronics corporation, Philips.

Inside a *maquila*

'You enter a spotless cavern housing two writhing conveyor belts,' I wrote at the time, 'queen insects tended by straight lines of rigid young women in colored bibs, perhaps a hundred seated down either side of each monstrous beast, fed with components at one end and churning out cardboard boxes like square eggs filled with TVs at the other... This is work that almost anyone can do and no-one with any real choice in the matter really wants... No-one lingers here. There is no human contact, no conversation. A canteen serving food during the break is deserted – two died recently of poisoning after eating in a *maquila* canteen down the road. We manage to talk to some of the women before their shift starts: mere children, they seem, in their bibs. Some of them are. Others are on the verge of tears. "I sleep and I work. I can do nothing else," one of them says. For this they are paid $30 a week and are not allowed to complain... Their young lives are scarred: materially, emotionally, physically and permanently. This is crude and scandalous exploitation. No amount of globaloney can obscure it.'

Resistance grows

Much the same impression was inescapable if you talked to any of the myriad citizens' groups or trade unions in Mexico City – the largest city in the world, and one of the most polluted. The Zócalo, the immense central square, was filled with wood smoke from the encampments of squatters from all over the country seeking to petition the President, whose official palace formed one side of the square – a metaphor for the state of formal politics in Mexico at the time, since it was usually uninhabited.

The impression that all was not exactly as the advocates of NAFTA would have it grew stronger the further south I traveled. I eventually reached Chiapas, dubbed by people in Mexico City as the 'crazy' state – the majority indigenous population make it more akin to neighboring Guatemala than to the rest of Mexico. On 15 September, Independence Day, I watched the celebrations in the old colonial capital, San Cristóbal de las Casas, high in the Chiapas mountains. The entertainers for the public show were all outsiders imported from elsewhere in the country. On the hillsides around the city, wood fires twinkled like stars pinpointing where communities of indigenous people looked down – or perhaps turned their backs – on the festivities in the valley below, from which they chose to remain conspicuously absent.

Just a third of the Mexican population, some 30 million people, still made their living from the land. But that was more than had lived in the entire country 50 years before. Mexico could not feed itself. The answer, according to the Harvard Business School graduates in Mexico City, lay with comparative advantage: sell tropical fruit to the Americans and buy cheap maize back. At the price of imported US maize, however, none of the eight million small farmers in Mexico whose lives and cultures depended upon cultivating it could possibly survive – they'd have to move to the cities and offer themselves up for work in the *maquilas*, like it or not.

'Here the "modern" way of industrial agriculture is not appropriate,' José Juarez Varela told me, in his Las Margaritas office near the Guatemalan border. He worked for the *Union de Ejidos de la Selva* (the Union of Rural Collectives in the Forest). 'We have no infrastructure, roads, communications, technical services, and the urban markets are a long way away. The land is extremely delicate and mountainous, unsuitable for machinery. Even agricultural reform [following the revolution that began in 1910] arrived here late. It wasn't until the 1950s that people started leaving the *fincas*, the great private estates, freeing themselves from debt-bondage and setting up *ejidos*, collective farms. They began to move into the forest and to grow whatever they were used to growing; bananas, maize, coffee.'

New markets

The *ejidos* joined together to form a Union. 'We learned a lot and we had a good time,' said José, 'but we weren't making a living.' The Union went through a crisis. Some felt like giving up. José and a small group toured the country in search of fresh ideas. In Oaxaca, the neighboring state to the north, they met up with a group of farmers who were producing coffee for the Max Havelaar fair-trade label in the Netherlands.

Cheap labor and the *maquiladoras*

From the mid-1960s onwards in Mexico – as in many other Central American countries – a new craze began for 'export-processing' assembly factories. Designated areas could operate outside the normal mass of regulations governing trade, importing raw materials or parts and exporting the product to the US. The proliferation of such factories around the world was one of the motive forces behind globalization. Most of the factories are either directly owned by transnational corporations or contracted to supply them. Much of the trade is between different parts of the same corporation.

Employment in such plants in Mexico, originally located for convenience on the border with the US, increased rapidly to nearly half a million by 1992 and nearer three million today. Over the years they have spread away from the US border and begun to recruit from Mexico's large indigenous population in the central highlands. The biggest single sector is transport (mostly automobiles), followed by electronics and textiles.

The main reason for establishing these factories was, of course, the cheap labor they could employ. Crude assembly work requires only the simplest of skills and minimal education – young women were considered particularly well-suited to this kind of work, provided they didn't get pregnant.

Organized labor was invariably banned. Many workers in the US complained about the impact on their own wage levels and employment of these 'runaway' jobs. The justification for them was that they increased employment for millions of Mexicans who were desperately in need of it. If working conditions were often very bad, they would improve with time.

In fact, wage levels in the *maquilas* – as in Mexico as a whole – fell relentlessly as the numbers employed in them rose, particularly following economic crises like the one in 1982, which was to prove the model for 'structural adjustment' policies around the world. ■

Hourly cost of labor and growth of employment in Mexican *maquiladoras*

Maquila workers (in thousands)
Average hourly labor costs in *Maquilas*

Year	Maquila workers	Avg hourly labor cost
1980		
1981		
1982		
1983		
1984		
1985		
1986		
1987		
1988		
1989		
1990		
1991		
1992		

Harry Browne and Beth Sims, *Runaway America*, Resource Center Press, Alburquerque, New Mexico, 1993.

On their return they decided to develop coffee production for niche export markets, including Max Havelaar. This meant a very different relationship with coffee buyers, cutting out the *coyote* middlemen and obtaining a guaranteed minimum price in exchange for guaranteed quality.

The Union bought an old cotton warehouse and converted it into a coffee storage and grading plant. Most of its production still went onto the ordinary commercial market, but after the collapse of world coffee prices in 1989 fair trade kept the Union alive. When I visited, it had just begun production for Twin Trading and Cafédirect in Britain, and for some specialist coffee traders in the US.

Down on the coffee farm

The following day we drove for three hours along broken roads to Cruz del Rosario, the nearest coffee-producing *ejido*. We had to announce our arrival at some distance from the village by blowing the truck horn three times – a reminder of growing tension and that intruders here were not always well-intentioned. We were greeted by a group of *ejidatarios* and eventually descended to the tropical forest in the valley below, where coffee bushes grew under the shade of forest trees. The ground was precipitous and had to be terraced. Rocks and boulders had to be shifted by hand. The farmers were moving to organic production which meant that no pesticides could be used to fend off disease – and no chemical fertilizers either. Compost was laboriously prepared from animal droppings and leaf-mould.

I wondered whether all this additional labor, even for a better price, really paid off. 'We are doing it for future generations,' replied Cirilo, who was taking me round.

This was the first time I had encountered fair trade on the ground in the South. I said to them that I would write about their work and perhaps, just perhaps, a few

NAFTA and all that

A North American Free Trade Agreement (NAFTA) was proposed by US President George Bush, President Carlos Salinas of Mexico and Canadian Prime Minister Brian Mulroney at a meeting in San Antonio, Texas, in June 1991. It formed part of a series of regional free-trade agreements throughout North and South America.

NAFTA finally came into effect on 1 January 1994. It makes provision for comprehensive trade liberalization with rules to remove 'distortions' of free trade and resolve trade disputes. It covers six broad areas:

● *Market access*: Average tariffs between Mexico, Canada and the US were already low, but high tariff barriers remained in the US and Canada against Mexican exports.

● *Trade rules*: Penalties and 'anti-dumping' – selling below cost to off-load surpluses or put competitors out of business – duty laws were imposed.

● *Trade in services*: Deregulation of a broad range of commercial services, including finance and transport.

● *Foreign investment*: Prefiguring later proposals for a worldwide Multilateral Agreement on Investment (MAI), NAFTA provides for 'national treatment' for all foreign investors.

● *Intellectual property*: Primarily a means of ensuring that patents held by corporations in the US or Canada are enforced in Mexico.

● *Dispute settlement:* This area was the most contentious during the negotiations, since it openly challenged national sovereignty and included the use of sanctions and fines.

Virtually all the important concessions, on investment, intellectual property and services, were made by Mexico. ■

more people would buy their coffee in the North – not all of us were of one mind with the corporate agenda. I had no doubt at all that what Max Havelaar and Twin Trading were doing there was important. The Union felt it had a real status of partnership. Without fair trade, small as it was, these people's lives would have been very much more difficult.

On 1 January 1994, and deliberately timed to coincide with the signing of NAFTA, an uprising would begin in Chiapas that continues to this day. It has become what the great Uruguayan writer Eduardo Galeano – a regular visitor – has styled 'the biggest siege in the world'. Once again, in Mexico City the people of Chiapas were derided, this time for seeking to make any connection at all between their obscure local difficulties and the grand designs of NAFTA.

A year or so later I came across José Juarez Varela from the Las Margaritas union office once again, this time in London. They had, he said, experienced an extremely difficult time; the uprising meant that they had lost one year's coffee harvest – a catastrophe. The Union had set up its own Café La Selva in a smart neighborhood of Mexico City, to sell their coffee and increase public awareness of their work. Fair and organic trade were even more important to them now, since their partners in the North had helped to keep them going through the disruption of the uprising and, more to the point, constant harassment by the Mexican military.

As for Mexico, within a year the country had been struck by a financial earthquake. An austerity program was imposed on millions, destroying their savings, cutting their wages or throwing them out of work altogether – so that Mexican banks could be bailed out of their misbegotten, NAFTA-related adventures. No such dispensation was offered to many thousands of small farmers who had taken the latest advice from the high priests of comparative advantage and borrowed heavily to invest in agricultural production for world markets.

Ciudad Juárez, for its part, is now notorious for industrial-scale criminal warfare of a quite shocking brutality, much of it related to narcotics. Which reminds me – Carlos Salinas, that elusive Harvard-educated President who knew so very well what was best for Mexico, who signed the NAFTA treaty but was never in his palace in the Zócalo, now lives in exile and disgrace. His brother was assassinated, but no doubt Salinas himself still has his hands on the fortune he made from oiling the works of the narcotics business. As for the PRI, it was finally ousted in the presidential elections of 2000 – by a former executive of Coca-Cola. Judge free trade by its results in Mexico and this is just about as good as it gets.

2 Coffee in Peru: life on the edge

What life is like for the first link in the chain of trade – the coffee farmers of the Tambopata river valley, on the border between Peru and Bolivia. How the coffee bean gets produced and why things never seem to work out.

IF TRADE IS a path, then fair trade is about the people it links together and who travel along it. Most paths carry an equal amount of traffic in both directions, or they would eventually fall into disuse. The trade in coffee, like Southern commodities generally, is different. Large quantities of coffee beans arrive at their final destination with Northern consumers, but only a tiny trickle of cash ever returns to coffee farmers in the South.

There is something rather curious about this. If we were to measure the value of something by the amount of human care and attention it receives, then by far the greatest value of the coffee bean would reside with the coffee farmer, whose working life is taken up with growing, picking, washing, drying and dispatching the thing. The very air is infused with the scent of fermenting coffee 'berries'. It's a safe bet that before being consumed every single coffee bean will have been touched many times by the hands of a coffee farmer. Thereafter, hardly anyone will see it, let alone touch it. Yet the less someone touches it, the more likely they are to profit from it. You might imagine that we were talking here about two entirely different species – the one with eyes, hands and feet, the other with mystical powers and a metaphysical identity.

Coffee has been for some time the fastest-expanding fairly traded product. It now takes a sufficiently large chunk out of the conventional market to have an impact on it. In many respects it is the ideal fair-trade product, and therefore not entirely typical. It is a 'pure' commodity that requires no additions and relatively simple processing, so the fairness of the trade is comparatively easy to assure. Small farmers account for a growing proportion of production – many of them own their land and work in cooperatives, thereby meeting one of the basic requirements of fair trade. And the world market for coffee has become more fastidious, closer to wine, with specialty coffees increasingly popular at the expense of the bland, uniform blends – partly as a result of food scares in the North, and possibly even because fair trade is having some effect.

'What has changed in my lifetime?' Abraham chuckled at the idea. He was 73 years old in June 1995 when I talked to him in San Juan del Oro, an old town on the lower eastern slopes of the Peruvian Andes, in the valley of the great Tambopata River, which flows into the Amazon Basin. During the previous ten years, Abraham had lived through the crossfire of a civil war between *Sendero Luminoso* ('Shining Path') revolutionaries and the Peruvian Army. Peace was only just returning. I was curious to know what he made of it all.

'I tell you this,' he said. 'The *cafeteleros*, the coffee farmers, were poor when we came here 40 years ago, and we are just as poor now. That has not changed at all.'

The earliest settlers here were Aymara- and Quechua-speaking peoples of the Peruvian Altiplano, who had lived for centuries around the desolate northern fringes of Lake Titicaca and were in urgent search of land. They began to make 'trouble', to form themselves into peasant unions. They were met with promises of reform. To relieve the pressure the Government built a road down into the forest that blankets the fragile, precipitous folds of the Andean escarpment to the east.

A new start

This was virgin territory, save for indigenous 'tribes' retreating ever-deeper into the forest as the road advanced. Here there was space, fertile soil and an escape from the relentless cold of the Altiplano. The prospect of a better life was pursued by landless people believing that a good living might eventually be made from growing coffee.

But the bounty of this majestic forest is not easily won, and it is won hardest of all by destitute colonizers such as these with nothing but their own labor to invest. From the road durable paths had to be fashioned up the sheer sides of the mountains. The sites for settlement had to be carefully selected. The cold at levels higher than 2,625 feet (800 meters), the heat and humidity at levels lower than 650 feet (200 meters) above sea level would kill the coffee plant.

Gregorio Gomez lived further up the valley from San Juan del Oro. 'I was born in the Sierra, the mountains, near Sandia,' he told me. 'When I was less than a year old, my parents brought me here. They came because there was not much of a life to be had in the Sierra, and there were a lot of people. Here in the valley, in those days, there were few people but plenty of land and things to produce, especially coffee.

'So I took it upon myself to educate myself, what we call "auto-education". Many people here have to get an education in this way. I went to institutions in Juliaca and Puno on the Altiplano, getting jobs where I could earn my keep and pay the fees. But still I kept in touch with my parents here, and with the *chacra* (farm). In fact, I built my own, slightly apart from my parents' one.'

Edi, Gregorio's young nephew, lived there with them. Edi's mother (Gregorio's sister) had suffered terribly for a year from an illness that crept from her feet through her body until it killed her – at the age of 20. They never knew its name.

As well as Spanish, Gregorio spoke the Quechua language of the Altiplano. This put him in a minority – most people in the valley spoke Aymara. His family mostly lived elsewhere so he was the only one who remained to care for his parents, Luis and Celestina, in their old age.

He was a member of the small San Isidro coffee-producers' cooperative and had just been elected vice-president of CECOVASA, the central union of nine cooperatives in the region which coordinated the marketing of almost all its coffee production.

The coffee business

Gregorio farmed coffee because there was no other living he could make. He was at one end of an enormous international industry dedicated to satisfying the consuming passions of affluent Northern drinkers. That industry generates billion-dollar profits which the people who produce the coffee itself never see. Unless things change, they never will. Although they – like some 20 million others in the tropical countries of the South – have worked all their lives for coffee, coffee has never worked for them.

So I arranged to follow Gregorio in search of a straight answer to a very simple question. At the price of a cup of coffee in London or Toronto, Sydney or New York, the 110-pound (50 kilos) sacks of coffee beans he produced in the Tambopata Valley were worth something in the region of $13,000 each. Yet, if he was lucky, he and his cooperative received just $70.

That's less than a 180th part.

Our first step along the way had to be upwards – quite a few steps upwards, as a matter of fact, to the steep, rainforest-coated slopes of the Tambopata River valley, where the coffee farmers lived and worked. It is hard to convey the sheer toil of climbing mountains through dense rainforest in humid tropical heat – something these farmers do all the time. Pole-axed by exhaustion after just a few minutes, I stood utterly bemused as a man scurried past me up the rough path, straining every sinew to push before him a wheelbarrow loaded with crates of Coca-Cola. Seldom had I been so struck by the motivating power of a global brand – although bottled soda was often the one relatively safe source of drinking water.

'Welcome to my *chacra*, my farm!' exclaimed Pamela when we eventually arrived, some two hours later. She took us by the hand and led us inside her house to a table decked with mandarins, papaya, jugs of juices, flowers, fresh herbs, simmering cups of cocoa. The one thing missing was coffee – if they drank it at all, the coffee farmers used it for relaxation in the afternoons.

'*Buenas tardes*, good afternoon,' said Pablo, Pamela's husband, after we had refreshed ourselves, introducing himself to my tape recorder. His darting eyes, mobile mouth and high-pitched croak made him seem roguish. But his laugh, like everyone's here, came straight from the soul.

'This is Pablo Cahuana Flores speaking. Member of the San Ignacio Cooperative. In the valley of the Tambopata River. Sandia. Department of Puno. Peru,' he shouted, as if reporting for duty. 'It is Friday.'

He trembled and was at a loss for words, transfixed by the machine. More to the point, no outsiders – and certainly no gringos like me – had ever visited him on his *chacra* before. He waited for a while for the words to come, then seemed to conclude that the best way

Who gets what

In terms of the final price paid by consumers for a jar of coffee, by far the largest chunk stays in the North. Retailers (mostly supermarkets) have a 'mark-up' of around 25 per cent – a good bit lower than on some other lines, because the coffee market is large and 'price sensitive', which means consumers have traditionally been reluctant to pay more for what looks like a standard product.

The largest single chunk – 55 per cent – is taken by the shippers and roasters, a euphemism for the giant food corporations like Nestlé or Kraft General Foods who control three-quarters of the trade. A good part of this is used to promote the key brands, like Nescafé or Maxwell House, as well as covering costs. To preserve freshness, coffee beans tend to be blended, roasted, ground and (where necessary) processed into 'instant' granules close to the final consumer.

The coffee jar Proportion received of the final price of a jar of coffee

Growers 10%

Exporters 10%

COFFEE

Shippers and Roasters 55%

Retailers 25%

The Coffee Chain Game, Oxfam.

Another ten per cent is taken by the exporters – the traders and dreaded 'middlemen' or 'coyotes' who organize the trade in the producing country.

This leaves just ten per cent for the producers themselves. As a group, and in terms of the number of people involved, they receive far less than anyone else.

It is, of course, to them that fair trade is chiefly directed. But within current structures there is a limit on what can be achieved. The real costs of insurance, shipping, roasting and distribution remain much the same, if not higher for fair trade because it is relatively small-scale and therefore cannot extract the advantageous contracts given to the big corporations, or benefit equally from the economies of scale.

That could be overcome quite simply, of course, if fair trade became bigger and more powerful in the marketplace. ∎

would be for us to see for ourselves. So he set off at high speed into the forest, beckoning us to follow and speaking fluently as he went.

The forest, he explained, had had to be thinned, while still preserving the shade needed by the coffee bushes, over an area of perhaps 7 acres (3 hectares) for each *chacra*. A platform had to be leveled to provide a drying area for the coffee, the loose soil soaked and compacted to form adobe walls for the two stories of the farmhouse; a building wide enough for a bed at each end, a table and bench in between, and not much else. A source of pure water had to be found. Finally, after the planting – first of essential vegetables and fruit for survival, then of the coffee itself – came the long, long wait: three years at least, tending the growing coffee plants 'like children' until the first fruits appeared. The hardships, the backbreaking labor without reward of these early years were still vivid in the memory of this place. They had never really gone away.

Forest product

'There they are,' he said, pointing to a clearing of felled trunks, forest litter and solitary papaya trees. A wooden aqueduct, perched on stilts, carried a trickle of water purposefully across the clearing into the forest beyond. Then I saw, nestling between two trunks, a bed of bright-green seedlings. 'They will serve me for 15 years,' said Pablo.

'Only 15?' I asked. The standard productive life of a coffee bush is more like 30 or 40 years.

'That's right. Lower down they last a little longer. But they produce less coffee. Over there, those plants are two years old. Up there, three. When the flowers come out in September it is as if the mountains were covered in snow, just like the Altiplano.'

We entered a grove of mature coffee bushes. They were planted about two meters apart. Dappled gray, skeletal stems, several of them to a bush, fanned out-wards from firm ground, clear and smooth save for a litter of leaves. The 'cherries', growing amid dark-green, glossy leaves from the stems of the outer fronds, turned from green to yellow and finally to red as they matured. They did, indeed, resemble small and unap-petizing cherries. Interspersed among the coffee bush-es were mandarin orange trees, brilliant with fruit.

Ahead we heard voices and there was Pamela again, beckoning frantically. She had draped a rough shawl from her shoulders to form two pouches around her waist. Half-a-dozen people, the men wearing num-bered soccer shirts of the latest design, emerged from the bushes.

They were *peones*, laborers. They came down from the Altiplano for about five months every year during harvest time and lived in a shed beside the farmhouse. Every *chacra* employed *peones*. Around the valley, at intervals through the forest, precious level ground had been cleared for them to play soccer on Sundays. They called Pamela and Pablo *dueños*, owners. There was, however, little to distinguish between them in terms of their visible wealth.

The pace of events began to quicken. Coffee 'cher-ries' flew in all directions. Mandarin oranges were plucked from the trees – a sack of 100 sold for less than one US dollar on local markets. There were bouts of hilarity as Pamela and her band of *peones* gave an exuberant exhibition of their daily drudgery.

Harvest time

This was harvest time for coffee – a critical time of year for the entire community, on which its fate for the com-ing year hinged entirely. Pablo was keen to impress upon me the seriousness of the task. 'We also produce coffee here for the *comercio alternativo*, for fair trade. We are careful to select only the best cherries for them, the ones that are perfectly ripe. It is a risk for us. There is only one day when they are perfect. If it rains on that day then they fall from the bushes and are lost. Sometimes it has rained for weeks during the harvest.'

The pouches were filled with cherries and we descended again towards the *chacra*. To one side of the farmhouse the wooden aqueduct poured crystal-clear water into a concrete tank. A vessel resembling a fat dugout canoe was filled with water. The cherries were unloaded into it and floated on the surface. They would sink slowly to the bottom as they fermented.

Beside this vessel was another similar one, filled previously, from which the fermented cherries were now removed and spread out to dry for a few hours. These cherries, by now reeking of fermenting fruit – a scent that remains with the coffee beans and I can smell to this day – were passed through a crude but effective de-pulper. Pour the cherries into a hob at the top, rotate the handle and hey presto! the soft fruit pulp falls out to one side while the hard coffee beans clatter down a tin chute to the other. The pulp would eventually be returned to the soil as compost. The beans still had a thick and resistant mucus coating. They were passed through more fresh water at least five or six times and literally scrubbed by foot or by hand. It was an extremely laborious process.

The drying process

The result – beans shining like polished peanuts – is called *café lavado*, washed coffee. These beans were spread out to dry in the sun for two or three days. Beans for the 'normal' market were placed on black synthetic material stretched directly over the ground. The *comercio alternativo* beans were on raised wooden platforms so that air could pass beneath them, making the drying process more effective. If rain threatened – and every night – the beans had to be gathered in and kept dry.

A husk still remained on the beans. Pamela and Pablo tested them as the drying proceeded by rubbing them between their hands to remove the husk and inspect the color and texture of the bean inside, until there was no sign of moisture and it had taken on a particular shade of gray-green. In this condition, still covered with the husk and known as *café pergamino*, the beans can be preserved for long periods without deteriorating – a quality that allows coffee to be produced as a cash crop even in such isolated spots as this.

We convened into a small circle to consider the implications of what we had seen. Gregorio conducted the interviews. We had been joined by Octavio Morales, a thin, solemn neighbor immaculately dressed and wearing a flat cloth cap.

'*Señor periodista inglés,*' Octavio began slowly in a deep, resonant and mournful voice, addressing me, the English journalist. 'We send greetings to your compatriots so far away and ask them to keep drinking their coffee. We want to thank you for coming to visit us here, the first journalist we have ever seen. Now you know for yourself how we must live, what a labor it is to produce coffee. But on the New York Coffee Exchange this morning the price has fallen to just $143 a sack.'

I was a little incredulous. How cold he possibly have known that?

'Yes,' continued Pablo, before I had a chance to ask. 'The price does not adequately reflect the work we put in, the costs we have to pay to maintain our families, employ *peones* and everything else. We produce coffee here of the highest quality, without using chemical fertilizers, herbicides or fungicides. Our coffee is completely organic and should receive a better price.'

I made a few simple calculations in my head. Assume that Pamela and Pablo would receive the equivalent of about $70 dollars, after the deduction of transport and processing costs, for each 110-pound (50 kilos) sack of *café pergamino* they were eventually able to sell – a pretty good price. If their *chacra* totaled about three hectares, and two hectares actually produced coffee at a good average (for here) of 20 sacks per hectare (10,000 sq km or 2.5 acres), then they should have been able sell a total of 40 sacks and receive a gross income of some $2,800.

Scarcely a princely reward, but still not far off the average income in Peru. However, out of this sum they still had to pay the wages and keep of the *peones* and the cost of transport by mule to the nearest coffee store. More to the point, three years previously they had received less than $20 per sack. Such prices were typical of the years between 1989 and 1993, when their income did not even cover the costs of production. The year before, after frost had killed part of the coffee crop in Brazil, a sack had sold for as much as $200 – a bonanza for Pamela and Pablo.

Survival mechanisms

To understand what this kind of uncertainty means for them, however, you have first to realize that the difference is not just between 'good' and 'bad' times. Living on the edge, as they do, your very survival hinges upon it. It's not so much a question of whether you have enough to eat – the forest is just about bountiful enough to make malnutrition avoidable. But, if your coffee harvest brings you in less than it costs you, if you have labored for a year without reward, then you will have nothing to pay for treatment for you or your children when sickness strikes, as it invariably does in places such as this – yellow fever is rampant. As a result, there are no doctors or medicines. The prevailing certainty becomes that if you get really sick you die – it's as simple as that. Whether or not you will be able to keep your children in school is doubtful. So there are not enough schools. The cumulative effect of all this continuing year after year, and of having to submit your life entirely to the whims of world coffee prices, is what powerlessness really means.

This also means that you take your chance to celebrate when you can. So our leaving ceremony became extremely protracted – suddenly everyone was equipped with compact cameras, bought with the bounty of the previous year's bonanza. We lined up by the *chacra*, by the drying coffee beans, the pulping machines, the coffee bushes and the papaya trees; we embraced different combinations of *peones, dueños*, families, friends, enemies, children and lovers, and we satisfied that universal longing to have our portraits made. Strange that I felt at all uneasy at leaving mine, my own 'soul', behind in this place – when I thought nothing of taking theirs with me.

We set off into the forest. We had been going just 15 minutes when we were stopped at a promontory by Daniel Limarche, who kept a shop. Inside was a cornucopia for sale: tinned fish, rice, Coca-Cola and a dozen bottles of real champagne. Daniel took me to a house where his niece was waiting, seated on a chair – a waif of a girl aged about seven. Her parents stood on each side of her. Daniel asked me if I would be her *padrino*, her godfather. He gave me a pair of scissors and asked me to cut off her hair – it would remain as a memento. Little Isabel began to weep as I cut her wispy strands.

The path descended in zigzags across the slopes of the valley. Giant trees stood over us; streams tumbled through dark, shaded air and the forest animals called their warnings – a sudden sound like a large drop of water falling into a still pond, or a slowly descending, derisive jeer. Out over the valley a condor glided patiently by. Treading a path where the stones had been worn smooth by the passage of human feet, we crossed sections that had been entirely swept away, the forest replaced by tangled roots, ugly naked earth baking dry and dusty in the sunlight – giant landslides. Some of them were still moving as we crossed.

It was tempting to push the ecological alarm button.

The price is wrong

The price for Robusta beans is fixed largely on the London Commodity Exchange; for the milder Arabica beans largely on the New York Commodity Exchange.

All sorts of things determine what that price is. There is, of course, 'supply' – the amount of beans available. The more there are, the lower the price will be. Then there is 'demand', or the amount of coffee people want to consume. The more of that there is, the higher the price will be. Since demand for coffee has been growing steadily, you'd have thought its price would have been rising. In fact it's been falling.

That's partly because, if prices start to rise, more bushes get planted by farmers but they don't start producing for three years, when there's a glut and prices fall. Occasionally a natural event – a frost killing the crop in Brazil, as it sometimes does – will restrict supply and prices will rise sharply.

Two things characterize the world price of coffee. The first is a dramatic variation from year to year, even day to day, making it very difficult for producers to plan ahead rationally. One reason for this is speculation. Some coffee is bought on 'futures' markets or as a 'hedge' against these kinds of fluctuations. This is supposed to 'stabilize' the market – in fact it does just the reverse, since speculators 'play' this market and shift large sums of money around very quickly.

The second characteristic is a long-term decline in the price of coffee. Unlike oil producers, coffee-producing countries do not work together to control production and therefore force prices up. The governments of these countries used to make agreements of this kind, but these collapsed in 1989. Periodic attempts to revive these agreements have so far met with little success. ■

Casino café The price of coffee on the New York Commodity Exchange 1970-99.

Frost damaged the Brazilian coffee crop in 1975 and 1994, causing sharp rises in price; droughts hit production in 1984, with a similar effect. The overall trend is visibly downwards.

International Coffee Organization, London.

This is an extremely sensitive environment – the headwaters of the Amazon. Four years previously I had been in the Brazilian Amazon just to the north, where concern had been mounting for some time at the increased rate that silt was being carried down into the Amazon Basin from the Peruvian escarpment, with unpredictable and possibly catastrophic environmental consequences throughout the region.

Fragile environment

Blaming the coffee colonists for this looked, at first sight, like a fairly straightforward matter. They were, after all, thinning the forest, weakening the delicate structures that hold a thin layer of topsoil to the slopes. Coffee is, like cash crops generally, a voracious consumer of the limited nutrients in the soil. All it takes is heavy rain and the soil erodes.

But the matter was not as simple as this. The whole of this region is, in geological terms, a very young environment, still in the process of formation. The soil of the Amazon rainforest itself derives largely from the silt eroded from these mountains; at least some is needed to replenish what is constantly washed into the Atlantic Ocean by the natural action of the giant river system. Looking to the summits of the mountains you could see light-green, healing scars made by earlier landslides caused quite naturally by the action of rain, lightning strikes or earth tremors.

What was not in doubt, however, was that the colonists were accelerating the natural process. They knew this well enough, losing as they did with every rainfall some of the fertility on which they relied for their very lives. Higher up the valley they told me that temperatures had begun to fall as the forest thinned – just as they had fallen in Brazil, which was why the Brazilian coffee crop had been affected by frost and the previous year's 'bonanza' had happened here.

No less in doubt was that it did not have to be this

way. For the coffee colonists operated, as they had always done, without any support or technical assistance of any kind. You did not have to be an expert – as I am not – to conclude that the most minimal precautions, such as terracing or a more informed approach to the thinning of the tree-cover, could have had a disproportionately beneficial effect. The problem was that people already on the brink knew that this, more even than healthcare or education, was beyond their means. There was no point whatever in advocating such things unless the resources were there to achieve them. Forty years of working for the conventional coffee trade had not produced these resources: no-one believed that it ever would. So everyone kept silent, hurrying without comment across the landslides, fearing perhaps that some gringo eco-imperialists might manage to banish them from their precious land altogether.

Since then Conservation International has arrived from the US and begun a project in the 'buffer' zone between the coffee farmers and the nature reserve in the Tambopata River Basin. The long process of registration for organic production has begun.

But if I were a coffee farmer I might be wondering why such palliatives must always arrive as unfamiliar offerings – with yet more instructions – from the source of the injustice itself, leaving my basic predicament intact. I'd be working for the day when I and my community had the power to decide things for ourselves; I'd know for certain that, in the long run and for my children's children, this is the only kind of change that works.

The long road to market

With disconcerting abruptness we emerged from the dimness of the forest path into brilliant light shimmering from the surface of a rough, dirt road. On the outer lip of the road an arc of tin-roofed, wooden huts perched over a precipice. A line of people sat in the shade on wooden benches watching the world, the coffee, an ancient bus, a small truck sprouting people like a vase, clatter by.

They called this place Punta de la Carretera, 'end of the road'. But this was just the beginning of the long, long voyage our coffee had yet to make to meet its market. An hour or so along the road was a rare sight, a large area of gently sloping ground and an expanse of tin roofs shining in the sun. This was Putina Punco, the first settlement of any real size – about 20,000 people – and the center for the coffee farmers of the Tambopata Valley. From here we visited *chacras* belonging to all four cooperatives – two big ones, San Jorge and Charuyo, with more than a thousand members each; two small ones, San Ignacio and Union Azata.

Coffee prices by radio

Near the river was a concrete square surrounded by warehouses. The co-op members brought their sacks here from great distances by mule – sometimes even on their backs – to be weighed, tested for quality, registered, stored and dispatched in large Volvo trucks. From an office to one side came the sound of a shortwave radio powered by a solar cell linked to a car battery. The *cafeteleros* could talk directly to Lima and learn the price of coffee that very moment on the New York Coffee Exchange. So that was where flat-capped Octavio had got the coffee price before we spoke on the farm earlier in the day.

One small co-op, the Union Azata, had lost a large chunk of its membership, which had once stood at 800 and was then no more than 120. *Chacras* had been abandoned, the investment lost, during the lean years between 1989 and 1993. Gregorio told me that Putina Punco had become a ghost town, losing 70 per cent of its population.

'Please tell your readers, David, so far away on other

continents,' said Hugo, a young and very bright official of Union Azata, 'that thousands of people here in this valley depend on the coffee they buy. You have seen how things are; how hard, how very hard we try to produce coffee of good quality for them. Tell them that we receive minimal payment for all our efforts. And tell all those ecologists, those very distinguished professionals, tell them to come and visit us here. Tell them that our forests are being extinguished and that we urgently, urgently need their help.'

'What we faced before the co-ops were founded,' added Gregorio, 'was having to sell all our coffee to a few powerful *comerciantes,* intermediaries. They committed a kind of violence against us. They treated coffee just like anything else, with ruthless self-interest and indifference to its quality, and the price they paid was very low.

'That didn't suit us. It didn't suit us at all. It was a very difficult struggle and we had to make many sacrifices, building our own warehouses, our own communications, transport and so on. However low the price of coffee may fall, we shall maintain our Co-op to the last, after all the sacrifices we made to set it up.'

I found the sheer isolation of this place intimidating. Sometimes I lay awake at night and it played on my mind. If it had rained at all heavily we would have been completely cut off, possibly for weeks. There was no electricity, no medicine, not a single doctor. Yellow fever stalked the houses.

So it was with some initial relief that I set off along the road out of Putina Punco taken by the coffee trucks.

We wound our way up the valley, climbing all the while. We stopped off at San Juan del Oro again, a slightly larger and older version of Putina Punco, with a gold mine in the mountains above, where Gregorio would work when times were bad with coffee. We filled the Nissan with petrol siphoned from barrels piled high in a store. An old man took me to see his run-down *chacra*, asserting repeatedly: 'What we need is technology!' Further along the road we called in at Gregorio's San Isidro co-op in Yanahuaya, then left him at his parents' *chacra*, where he had work to do on the coffee harvest.

Onto the Altiplano

And so, eventually, we set off for the Altiplano. As we climbed, the forest gave way to scrub and then arid rubble. The higher we climbed the more the mountains seemed to loom over us, the more precipitous became the fall to the river ever-further below us. At the head of one valley was an amphitheater of astonishing grandeur, terraces cut by the Incas into the side of the mountain and still used to carry the weight of the road, which zigzagged straight upwards. It proved wise not to look over the edge, as if from an aircraft, at the receding pins of light in the deepening dusk on the valley floor. This, I was told, was where *cafetelero* Abraham had lost one of his sons.

The cold became intense, penetrating, as darkness engulfed us. With the altitude my breathing began to labor, my head to spin and ache, the pain amplified by violent blows against the side and roof of the lurching vehicle, which I was helpless to prevent. We could see nothing except the dusty track ahead, illuminated in the head lamps. I envied the inanimate coffee bean that came this way too.

We stopped at what at first appeared to be a bright doorway in space. Slowly, as my eyes adjusted to the radiant starlight, I could see the shadows of buildings and, behind them, snow peaks near enough to touch. The summit of the pass. We had climbed for six hours, from 800 to 5,000 meters, more than 16,000 feet above sea level.

The journey was still far from over, though we climbed no more. I recall a reflection of stars dancing on the surface of Lake Titicaca, and a bright strip of orange light in the distance – Juliaca, our destination and the end of the stars. After a day and a night on the road, dawn was not far away.

Juliaca is built from the materials of the flat earth on which it stands and it was not always easy to tell whether the buildings were rising up from it or subsiding back into it. The streets were jammed with rickshaws and markets. The town had two great attractions for the coffee producers: electricity to drive a processing plant and banks for the export business.

So it was here that the Central Office of Agrarian Coffee-producing Co-operatives of the Valleys of Sandia (CECOVASA) had its base. The coffee trucks from Putina Punco arrived in the yard and unloaded their cargo into a warehouse. At the end of the warehouse was a line of green machines made in Brazil and Colombia. The first shook out the crudest impurities in the *café pergamino*: stones, wood and other relics of the valleys. From here the bean passed into a cylindrical mill which removed its husk – and, I was later to discover, a good part of its taste as well. Pergamin coffee beans are not uniform and the husks are liable to more rapid decay than the beans, so are not what world markets require. Finally, the naked bean emerged; a small, unprepossessing lozenge in two fused segments known as 'green' coffee.

Export grading

A stack of four more sieves, shaking violently, graded the green beans by size. Only the largest were considered suitable for export – as in most coffee-exporting countries, inferior beans were sold for domestic consumption only. Something like 20 per cent of the beans failed to pass muster for export. Finally they ran the gauntlet of a conveyor belt set between a line of hired hands who completed a manual grading process, leaving only beans akin to jewels.

The previous year CECOVASA had exported almost 22,000 sacks of green coffee, valued at some $3.5 million. Until the early 1980s all coffee exports from Peru had to go through government agencies, which had traditionally relied on the US market. Since then – and with a marked improvement in the doubtful reputation for quality of Peruvian beans – new markets had been developed in Japan and Europe, which now bought 80 per cent of their coffee.

'We have good news,' said Pablo, the manager, sitting in an office with fair-trade posters covering the walls. 'The price is rising. Over $150 on the New York Exchange today. Rumors of another poor harvest in Brazil. An announcement expected from the Brazilian Government shortly. This is a relief for us. We have been holding on, waiting to make sales because we thought the price would rise – but instead it fell.'

The green coffee now had to travel in rented 20-ton trucks for two days across a mountainous desert down to the coast, then north to Callao, Lima's seaport. Time, graciously, insisted that I fly from Juliaca to Lima. In Callao an official in a sharp black uniform plunged a stiletto blade into some of the sacks as they arrived, searching for cocaine. No-one had said much about it – and I had not asked – but everyone clearly knew well enough that when the coffee trade slumped the coca trade flourished. A gang of laborers lined a container with brown paper and filled it with 250 sacks to make up the standard 'lot'. The doors were sealed. The beans would not see the light of day again until they reached their destination; through the Panama Canal to Europe or North America; across the Pacific to Japan and Australasia. I gave them a friendly pat to see them on their way. Meanwhile, the coffee price in New York fell.

3 Cocoa in Ghana: a way of life

How much cocoa means to Ghana and the people who produce it. What 'structural adjustment' policies do in practice, not least to the cocoa farmers themselves. Why the gains they've made from being able to organize themselves have been lost in other ways.

A COMMON FEATURE of many Southern countries is that they depend very heavily indeed on a single export crop. Even a huge and relatively wealthy country like Brazil relied until quite recently on a sequence of single export commodities, shifting in turn from sugar to rubber to coffee and soy beans, but never sustaining

them together so that bad years in one might be balanced out by better years in another. One reason for this is the way 'comparative advantage' on world markets makes one crop temporarily very much more profitable than another, thereby encouraging a herd instinct – particularly in powerful landowners – to switch en masse between them and promoting extremely vulnerable 'monoculture' economies.

Another aspect of this phenomenon relates less to abstract theories of 'comparative advantage' than to the past, since the economies of colonies were constructed to suit the colonial master. Whether it was cotton from India, spices from Southeast Asia, gold from South Africa or cocoa from Ghana, the 'value' of these commodities was conceived entirely in Northern terms, with little regard to the long-term benefits or otherwise to local people.

From this it has followed that the economic 'spread

effect' – bringing greater prosperity to the population as a whole – of commodity exporting has always been extremely limited. By and large, the value that was added to a basic raw material by its processing, manufacture and commercialization was retained very firmly in the North – and with it the capital for future development. The advent of independence has done little to alter the basic shape of this process. Particularly in Africa, many countries remain as dependent today on a single export crop as they were in colonial times.

The consequences of this reach deep into postcolonial societies. Not least, their governments come to rely very heavily on taxing exports to generate revenues. This consolidates the political influence of the world trading system over these societies, whether they have achieved self-determination and political independence or not.

In recent years the political impact of this economic relationship has been made more overt by the debt crisis. Northern creditors have been able to insist not merely on repayment, but on precisely how the economies of debtor countries are to be run. Their prescription, 'structural adjustment', has become entirely formulaic: the promotion of exports, the devaluation of currencies to make exports even cheaper, the removal of regulations, the withdrawal of democratic control, the cutting of public expenditure on basic services like education and healthcare, the privatization of public assets: the free-trade agenda.

Failed agenda

It is now becoming clear that this agenda has failed. To get an idea of how and why this has happened we take a closer look at one crop and one country. Ghana and cocoa have been synonymous for years. One of the abiding ironies is that the final product, chocolate, is not eaten by most Ghanaians.

Heat and light begin to settle over Accra before six

in the morning. It is the kind of heat where the cotton of your shirt already sticks to your skin by eight in the morning... and you search for a breath of breeze blowing off the Atlantic.

Out in the field

I have arranged with Sam Nyako of the Ghanaian Cocobod (cocoa marketing board) to travel upcountry to the Cocoa Research Institute in Tafo and to the Agricultural College which trains the board's extension officers, who help farmers improve their cocoa production. It will give me a chance to have a look at what Ghana does to sustain a crop that is a vital part of its economic well-being. Also, to find out firsthand about the effects of the economic liberalization process, designed with World Bank and International Monetary Fund (IMF) help, that is having a dramatic impact not only on cocoa farmers but on all Ghanaians.

Accra is just waking up as we pull out of town and start the journey towards Tafo, a town located in the upcountry, about four hours' drive to the northeast. The combination of the cooler height and the breeze blowing in through the window of the four-wheel-drive provides welcome relief.

As we climb we are treated to a spectacular view of the Accra plain spread out below, the shimmering Atlantic beyond. Long lines of school children in brown tunics, pants and neat yellow shirts stretch out along the road all the way to the next hilltop. They meander past Ghana's 'informal sector' setting itself up on the roadside to sell anything it has that anyone could conceivably want, or afford, to buy: huge yams, *fou fou* (porridge), soups (the Ghanaian name for stews, or indeed almost any food), toilet paper, batteries, pens, lottery tickets – you name it.

As we drive north Sam fills me in on the history of the Ghanaian Cocobod. It has its roots in the colonial buying monopoly set up by the British at the time of the

Second World War. This was in response to African complaints that they were getting ripped off by the expatriate firms whose agents monopolized the purchase of the cocoa crop. The early history of cocoa production here is marked by a series of struggles in which farmers got together to hold back the sale of their crops and force up the price.

While the declared purpose of the board was to shield farmers from speculators and price fluctuations, it never in fact did this. For the British, and later for independent Ghanaian Governments, cocoa proved too tempting a source of public finance to allow a fair price. Proceeds from cocoa had to underwrite the plans of Kwame Nkrumah for ambitious education, health and industrial projects. So heavy export taxes and other tariffs kept producer prices low. 'We compensated for this at the Cocobod, at least partially, by a series of free services to farmers, including subsidized fertilizers, pesticides and herbicides, free agricultural extension services, research and development of the best cocoa hybrids for Ghanaian conditions, free saplings, even labor to help at busy times on the farm,' Sam says. The argument was that despite low prices farmers were getting back some value in services.

Market fluctuations

But this did not prove enough to sustain the cocoa economy. When the bottom first dropped out of the cocoa market in the 1970s (as it did more recently in 1999-2000), prices tumbled from almost $4,800 a ton to less than a third of that. With farmers getting less than 40 per cent of the world price from the Cocobod, this was a significant blow. Many farmers stopped producing cocoa altogether or switched to food crops like maize and cassava that fetched more reliable prices.

The situation worsened with the Sahelian drought that hit West Africa in the early 1980s. By 1983 conditions were so dry that a series of disastrous bush fires swept across Ghana's cocoa-growing country. Production plummeted. In 1972 Ghana produced nearly a third of the world's cocoa. A decade later this had fallen to just 12 per cent. With Ghana, like most of sub-Saharan Africa, staggering under a huge debt burden, the collapse of cocoa left the country teetering on the edge of bankruptcy.

It was at this point that the World Bank and IMF stepped in with a structural-adjustment package to 'rescue' the country's economy. If you read all the official literature you will conclude that this has been a tremendous success. For cocoa this meant a dramatically downsized Cocobod and significantly higher prices for farmers. All sounds like good stuff.

As we pull through the gates of the Cocoa Research Institute in Tafo I get an idea of the effort that has been made to sustain vital cocoa yields. The station dates from colonial times and has a range of laboratories, experimental farms, nurseries and so many PhDs that Sam jokingly refers to them as 'doctors without nurses'. It concentrates on basic plant science, with special attention to cocoa as a small-farmer crop. It has pioneered inter-cropping, allowing small farmers to grow food crops in the three-to-five years it takes cocoa trees to produce their first pods.

At Tafo they have developed a hybrid cocoa, marrying the traditional type to a new Amazonian variety from Brazil with an eye to taste, bean count, yield per acre (0.405 hectares), disease resistance and quickness to maturity. The old type yields only one crop after five years whereas the new variety yields two crops after just three years – a vital difference for marginal small farmers. The Institute feels their hybrid is the most productive for West African conditions.

We move from building to building meeting with the plant people, the bug people, the disease people, the cocoa byproducts division and finally the economist. It quickly becomes clear that, while the Institute has been vital in sustaining cocoa as a small-farmer crop, there is a constant tension between its expensive, scientific, agrochemical approach and what the farmers can afford to do in the field.

We drive to the Cocobod's Agricultural College at Bunso. Here the mood is decidedly more downbeat. Structural-adjustment reforms have bitten deep into the agricultural extension service. Overall, the Cocobod has

Chocolate follies – a brief history

The first known use of the cocoa bean was to make a spicy (not sweet) chocolate drink and dates back to the Mayan empire (250-900AD) in what is today southern Mexico and Guatemala. It was a symbol of sanctity and evoked both fertility and prosperity. Thence it spread with the Aztec Empire to the North, where beans were also used as currency. Chocolate was not immediately to the taste of the Spanish conquistadores, until sugar was added to accommodate the passion of Europeans for sweetness. They made chocolate into a tablet that was readily transportable to Europe. The fanatical Charles the Second of Spain reportedly sat sipping chocolate while observing victims of the Inquisition being put to death.

For some time chocolate remained a mysterious luxury item largely confined to the Iberian peninsular in Europe. Slowly it spread with trade across the continent. Experts debated whether it cooled over-heated or heated cooler passions. The Marquis de Sade's status as one of the earliest-known 'chocoholics' added a certain spice to its reputation.

With the invention of the cocoa press by the Dutchman Van Houten in the late 19th century, cocoa butter could be extracted from the beans, leaving a powder of cocoa solids. A vast new confectionery industry came into being. The Cadbury company brought the press to England and was quickly joined by Rowntree, together with Milton Hershey and then Forest E Mars in the United States.

Today, less than two per cent of cocoa comes from Mexico. World production shifted to West Africa at the end of the 19th century. The belief in Ghana is that the cocoa seedlings were smuggled in by a Ghanaian carpenter named Tetteh Quarshie in 1878. Ghana was the world's largest producer between 1910 and 1979.

Chocolate companies, buyers and development agencies like the World Bank encouraged a number of new countries to begin producing the 'miracle' commodity. Asian countries like Malaysia and Indonesia set up large plantations, while Brazil and other Latin American countries also increased their production. The result was an increase in supply – and a fall in price. Most of the plantations have not, however, been a success and Malaysia is withdrawing from the market. Plantations are still rare in West Africa. ■

dropped from some 100,000 employees to less than 10,000. In areas like extension the effects have been dramatic. Workloads have doubled and Alfred Nortley, one of the College's administrators, reports that 'morale is low. It is almost impossible to do your job, and the farmers are starting to complain quite bitterly.' The College is not currently training extension workers at all as there are simply no jobs. This may also explain the frustration back at the Institute. It is the extension workers who are charged with transferring the Institute's agronomy on to the farmers.

Cuts at Cocobod

No-one would seriously argue there was no fat in the Cocobod and cuts weren't needed. Many of its workers and functions were of marginal utility and at the cost of a better price to cocoa farmers. Today the price farmers get has risen to 50 per cent of the international price, with the Board committed to go even higher, to 65 per cent or 70 per cent. But structural adjustment is turning out to be a blunt instrument, cutting away many of the beneficial services to farmers the Cocobod did perform. Put this together with the other effects of structural adjustment and it is by no means clear that cocoa farmers – supposedly one of the main beneficiaries of the IMF/World Bank reforms – are much better off. Not only are inputs more expensive, but the cost of living for ordinary Ghanaians has skyrocketed. In all my time in Ghana I never heard anyone say anything positive about the impact of structural adjustment.

As we head back towards Accra my conversation with Sam shifts to other changes in the farmers' lives. The user fees in education and health have been particularly difficult. There are lots of stories about those who simply can't afford schooling. For most, higher education is inconceivable. Sam is particularly aware of the effects on health costs. He recounts stories of people turned away from hospitals in the middle of the night, forced to carry desperately sick family members back home either because they lacked the money or just because the banks were closed and they couldn't get their hands on the cash. Sam shakes his head and stares out of the window pensively. The words come slowly. 'Ghana never used to be like this,' he says.

To help shore up public revenues and meet Ghana's obligations to international creditors, as well as cover the high cost of imports resulting from the devalued *cedi*, the IMF/World Bank package called for a value-added tax (VAT) to replace all other sales taxes. The idea was to shift some of the tax burden away from cocoa and encourage production. But when the Government tried to bring in the tax at 17 per cent even the usually peaceful Ghanaians took to the streets in protest. They cried '*kume preko*' ('kill me quickly' – as opposed to the lingering death of structural adjustment) and the police obliged, gunning down several demonstrators. But the outcry was so great that the Government was forced to back down.

The cocoa co-op

The headquarters of Kuapa Kokoo (cocoa co-op), is in the Ashante capital of Kumasi – Ghana's second-largest city and the heart of cocoa country. Its offices occupy the two floors of a large villa-like building. The number of comings and goings is a good hint that this is where a lot of the cocoa action in town takes place. Despite the obvious busyness, this is no stuffy office. Cocoa farmers sit around chatting, and some have spent the night on the floor of a large sleeping room: testament to the comfort and sense of ownership of Kuapa members.

Kuapa has several faces. It is at once a farmers' union, a cocoa-purchasing company and a trust fund for its members. It started back in 1993 when Nana Frimpong Abebrese, a far-sighted farmers' representative on Cocobod, saw that the partial privatization of internal purchase might leave cocoa farmers at the mercy of unscrupulous private companies. He feared a return to the bad old days when middlemen-buyers and moneylenders preyed on farmers. The best way to avoid this, he surmised, was for the farmers to organize themselves to collect, sell and profit from their own cocoa. To do this the union had to set up its own purchasing company, as under Ghanaian company law it was illegal for a cooperative to buy and sell cocoa without a license from the Cocobod.

How it works

A local society is the basic building block of Kuapa and can vary from dozens to hundreds of members. When it started, Kuapa had 22 local societies – the number has now mushroomed to 160. Kuapa Kokoo say that they now count on more than 30,000 members spread right across Ghana's cocoa belt. Kuapa Kokoo relies on committed and energetic staff. The current head of the Gender and Society Development activities is a woman, Anna Antwi, who barely mentions the cocoa-chemistry degree and training in cocoa agronomy that lies behind her work with her department, which passionately advocates community organization, good meeting practices, women's rights and support activities.

Blending the desirable and the necessary is crucial for a fledgling grassroots organization such as Kuapa, which needs to avoid becoming a voice in the wilderness or falling into business-as-usual cronyism. Support workers spend a good deal of time on the road strengthening existing societies or establishing new ones. Most Kuapa Kokoo workers appear to balance a commitment to the cocoa farmers' cause with caution born of the realization of the importance of the annual crop to the whole country. Nana Anson, a former Society Development Officer, is clear: 'Ghana has developed on the back of the cocoa farmer: roads, hospitals, schools,

Trade and development – no automatic link

Orthodox economics suggest that the more a country trades – and in particular, exports – the greater the well-being of its people. Even by some very traditional measures, like economic growth, this is very far from always being true. In 1997, for example, Russian exports (mostly of commodities like oil) were growing rapidly but its economy grew by just 0.4 per cent. Meanwhile, wages fell by almost a half in that year alone, after seven years during which inequality had doubled and male life expectancy declined by more than four years. The wealth of trade disappeared into the pockets of an élite (much of it criminal) that was plugged into the circuits of economic globalization.

Taking broader measures of human development, the picture is no less ambiguous. The UN's Development Program (UNDP) has devised what it calls a ' human development index' (HDI) which includes broader measures of well-being – education, health, gender, inequality – than mere money.

It goes on to suggest what level of well-being might reasonably be expected from the material wealth of a particular society. Some relatively poor societies – like the Indian state of Kerala – achieve very much higher levels of well-being than might be expected, while some relatively rich societies – like Saudi Arabia and even Switzerland – achieve very much less. For these latter there is a 'shortfall' on the HDI, which characterizes a quite large number of societies around the world.

Combing three measures of development – exports, average income and the HDI shortfall – shows wide variations. In some places, like Singapore and Mauritius, strong growth in exports corresponds with rapid growth in incomes and marked reductions in the HDI shortfall. In others, like Pakistan or Uganda, exports and incomes have grown quite quickly but the HDI shortfall has been reduced very little.

The reasons for this are associated above all with government policies and political decisions. ■

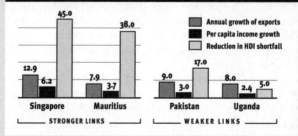

Trade, growth and well-being 1985-97 (per cent)

- Annual growth of exports
- Per capita income growth
- Reduction in HDI shortfall

	Singapore	Mauritius		Pakistan	Uganda
Annual growth of exports	12.9	7.9		9.0	8.0
Per capita income growth	6.2	3.7		3.0	2.4
Reduction in HDI shortfall	45.0	38.0		17.0	5.0

STRONGER LINKS | WEAKER LINKS

Human Development Report 1999, UNDP.

everything comes from cocoa.'

It is ironic that it is the structural-adjustment program, so unpopular throughout Ghana, that has given the space for Kuapa to exist. It forced the Cocobod to give up its monopoly on internal purchase, allowing the farmers themselves to take over this function. The Cocobod has technically kept its word: producer prices are rising as a share of the market price beyond 55 per cent or even the 60 per cent promised. But, while farmers are enthusiastic for increased prices, all workers in the sector are cautious about the total liberalization of cocoa marketing being pushed by the World Bank and the IMF.

What happens elsewhere

Other countries in West Africa, such as Cameroon, Nigeria and to a lesser extent Côte d'Ivoire, that are opening up cocoa purchase and export to external companies, have suffered a perilous deterioration in quality, worsening prices and a rush for quick profit. 'Ghana produces the best cocoa in the world and we get a premium on the price. It is the Cocobod's Quality Control Division that is largely responsible for maintaining these standards,' cautions Nana Anson. He is also quick to underline other deleterious effects of adjustment policies on farmers, such as the collapse of a once-vital rural-credit system due to imposed reforms. Most farmers can no longer meet the stringent criteria for collateral demanded by the banks and end up either without vital credit or borrowing from private money-lenders and purchasing companies at rates of up to 100-per-cent interest.

It is not hard to figure out the attraction of Kuapa for Ghana's cocoa farmers. Not only do they run their own show, but it's a much better deal. For the last three years in a row, with other new companies barely trading, Kuapa paid a bonus to every farmer averaging 500 *cedis* per bag over and above the Cocobod price.

An additional 300 *cedis* per bag went into the coffers of the local village societies for their own work and activities. At the end of the year, four representatives from each society – two women and two men – come to Kumasi for a big meeting to divide up the year's profits. In the last two years this has amounted to 700 *cedis* per bag. This is a matter of a few US cents and may seem like small potatoes – but for a hard-pressed farmer it can make a big difference.

About 11 per cent of Kuapa's output is sold to fair-trade organizations in Europe – these include the Day Chocolate Company and the Body Shop, which uses fair-trade cocoa butter in its line of natural cosmetics. The British-based fair-trade organization, Twin Trading, helps orchestrate these arrangements. However, they are by no means assured, as I learn when I meet the no-nonsense Managing Director of the marketing company. He expresses some fear that fair-trade organizations may not buy the full amount of cocoa that Kuapa has allotted for them this year.

Fair-traders

On what they do purchase, these fair-traders return a premium to Kuapa which is based on a minimum price for the beans of $1,600 – compared with current market prices of about $800 – and a 'social premium' of $150 per ton*. I assume that this premium goes right back to the farmers, but am pleasantly surprised when it's explained to me that it goes into a trust fund to support community infrastructure. Already more than $300,000 has been accumulated and the Kuapa Kokoo Farmers' Trust takes proposals from different communities for such things as health centers, water bore holes, improvements to schools and credit schemes. There is an on-going program to sink a clean-water bore hole in each Kuapa Kokoo village

1 US ton = 2,000 lbs. 1 metric tonne = 2,240 lbs/1,000 kg

that doesn't have one yet.

Kuapa's society development team also counts on a sustainable-agriculture officer to teach integrated pest management, and has a proactive program to ensure the empowerment and financial well-being of women members. The officers are quick to point out that a large number of farmers can no longer afford expensive imported pesticides, now that adjustment policies have removed price subsidies.

Cocoa is, worldwide, one of the most highly sprayed of all food crops. So going at least partially 'organic' is a practical as well as a philosophical step. The pride in the quality of the cocoa is universal, however, and of course popular with the fair-trade organizations who need '*papa pa*' – 'the best of the best'. The license plates of the Kuapa trucks have '*papa pa*' neatly inscribed on all of them.

Cocoa is like a lot of other Southern export crops. In the lingo of the economists it lacks structural links, or 'spin-offs', to the domestic economy. Aside from the obvious income accruing to individual farmers, or going into public expenditure, very little by way of job creation or industrial activity results from growing cocoa. Increasingly, producer countries are doing some of the processing before the cocoa is exported, which at least provides some extra employment.

Home-grown chocolate

In Ghana there is a small chocolate industry producing an excellent range of high-cocoa Golden Tree chocolates in the port cities of Tema and Takoradi. But these are successfully kept out of the North by high tariff walls – 34 per cent in Europe – and poor economies of scale. Most of this chocolate is consumed in the very small domestic market. It is a luxury item, out of the reach of most Ghanaians. There are ambitions to build a regional market for Golden Tree, but even if these are successful markets will remain limited by low incomes and cheaper competition from the Big Chocolate of multinationals.

So it is not unreasonable for governments to tax exported cocoa as a way of spreading some of the cocoa wealth to meet the needs of the rest of society. In West Africa, the big producing countries – Ghana and Côte d'Ivoire – have done this to a point where the small cocoa farmer bears too much of the burden of state expenditure. This endangers the sustainability of the cocoa economy and now the pendulum is swinging back, to give farmers a better deal on their crop. The 'spread-effect' is more significant where cocoa remains a small-holder crop than it is on the agro-chemical plantations of Indonesia, where workers make about one dollar a day.

Structural-adjustment straitjacket

While it is important for farmers to get a decent price it is also important for the governments of the South not to have their fiscal hands tied when trying to meet such basic needs as heath, education, farmer-support and infrastructure maintenance. Unfortunately, their hands are being tied by structural adjustment. In Ghana this is compounded by the problem of aging and often absentee cocoa farmers.

Another potential spin-off is the spectacular number of byproducts that can be derived from cocoa: fertilizer, animal feed and soap – as well as a range of cakes, biscuits and jams from cocoa powder. These last are being experimented with at the cocoa research station in Teme, which is also producing a gin and a brandy made from the 'sweatings' of the cocoa beans during the fermentation process. While none of these things is likely to add up to much in terms of the Gross Domestic Product, they are an invaluable part of the survival economy in which cocoa farming is rooted – the complete utilization of the crop helps sustain a way of life and the social-security system of rural Ghana.

4 Bananas in Guatemala and the Caribbean: seeking perfection

War breaks out over the world's largest herb. Why the World Trade Organization (WTO) promotes slavery and environmental insanity. Amidst all this, what chance for the perfect, fairly traded and organic banana?

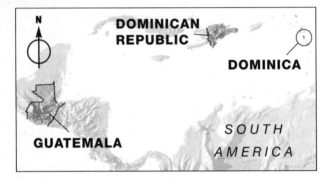

FAIR TRADE HAS to learn how to flourish in a hostile world. Convention dictates that trade must engage from time to time in skirmishes or wars. Any resemblance to an honorable duel vanishes, however, when one of the parties turns up with a machete and the other with an array of modern weaponry.

From time to time two bloated brawlers may, nonetheless, find themselves lumbering into battle, often over a seemingly trivial matter. Such has been the case for a good while now with the United States and the European Union (EU). The matters at issue have ranged from aircraft noise to beef, but the noisiest spat of recent years broke out over bananas growing in the tiny Windward Islands of the eastern Caribbean.

Every war needs a warmonger, and in the Banana War of 1999 that role was assumed by one Carl H Lindner Jnr. He heads the American Financial Group, which includes among its assets Chiquita Brands International of Cincinnati – along with the Dole Food Company and Del Monte Fresh Produce, one of the Big Banana corporations that control most of the world's trade in the fruit. In mid-1999 Mr Lindner claimed that $500 million was what he was owed on account of the European banana 'regime', and he wanted the US Government to get it back for him.

Evidently, Carl H Lindner Jnr is a man of substance. His personal wealth is estimated at $830 million, much of it dredged from the murky waters of Savings and Loans institutions in the US. A strict Baptist who never drinks, smokes or swears, he has a habit of handing out little white cards with gold-embossed aphorisms on them, such as: 'I like to do my giving while I'm living so I know where it's going.' Though he prefers the Republicans and lent Robert Dole a corporate jet during the 1996 presidential campaign, when he saw the electoral tide flowing towards the Democrats he slipped Bill Clinton a quick $500,000.

A few days later the Banana War between the US Government and the EU, that had been simmering away for years, duly boiled over. If, as a result of it, Mr Lindner were to get the $500 million he reckoned he was owed, then he would have made a handsome return on his investment in Bill Clinton.

Warped world

Welcome, then, to the warped world of bananas. Or rather, to the bent business of international trade in bananas. There is a difference. For the Banana War was officially being waged between two regions – the US and Europe – that grow almost no bananas at all. On the other hand, the world's two largest banana producers – Brazil and India – grow them largely for domestic consumption and have little to do with the international trade.

Almost everywhere in the tropics the fruit of the

world's largest herb has been adopted by small farmers as a prolific source of nutritious food. The banana, *Musa sapiculum*, is a remarkable plant structured rather like a giant leek. There are many varieties growing in myriad settings, from a few plants for household consumption to plots for local markets. They grow fast; the stem dies back once the fruit is harvested, but already the next 'follower' is preparing to take over. Carefully tended, on the right soil, in the right climate and with minimal inputs, a plot of a couple of acres (about one hectare) can produce several bunches, with 100 to 200 bananas on each of them, every week, all year round, for 30 years.

International trade

Less than a quarter of all the world's bananas, however, gets mixed up in international trade, and it's only when they do that they encounter the banana business, where things can get a bit twisted. Just one variety, Dwarf Cavendish or Gran Enano, is preferred by the world banana trade. On plantations across Central America, northern Latin America, parts of Africa and Asia, vast numbers of clones are planted out on flat land, much of which is swept by hurricanes. The deforested land on which they grow is drained and degraded. The plants are subjected to ceaseless treatment by toxic chemicals. Their unripe fruit are cut green, fragile and inedible from the stem, the bunches strung like carcasses to cable ways that carry them off for scrubbing with more chemicals. Graded and packed into boxes, dispatched in refrigerated ships ('reefers') to Europe and North America, the hapless fruit is then ripened for supermarkets and conjured into an image of 'quality' that people around the world who live in ignorance of the truth wish to consume in ever-increasing billions.

This is the 'dollar' banana that accounts for 80 per cent of the fruit we eat in the North and is controlled by Chiquita, Dole and Del Monte. They in turn are subsidiaries of conglomerates, like Mr Lindner's American Financial Group. Together, the Big Three constitute an oligopoly that controls the supply of bananas, fixes prices and has an inordinate love of secrecy. When, in May 1998, the *Cincinnati Enquirer* had the temerity to publish an exposé of how Chiquita actually operates, the company sued. It wasn't that the reports were inaccurate. Quite the reverse – they'd made use of the corporation's internal voice mail and thus violated its right to privacy. The newspaper issued an abject apology, paid Chiquita an undisclosed sum (thought to be in the region of $10 million), a journalist was sacked and prosecuted and the reports removed from its website. You bet, the Big Three mean business.

Lomé Convention

On the other side of the low-intensity Banana War was Europe and its import regime. In a Byzantine web of quotas, licenses and tariffs, the EU – the world's largest importer – was protecting the banana industries of its former colonies. These are grouped into the ACP (Africa, Caribbean, Pacific) countries to which Europe made firm commitments in the Lomé Convention of 1975, renewed four times. The Lomé agreements are by no means a passport to prosperity for the ACP countries. But banana exports are critical to a number of ACP economies, and particularly to the Windward Islands of Dominica, St Lucia, St Vincent and Grenada. Growers here are paid roughly double the price, and incur roughly three times the production costs, of the 'dollar' banana.

The renewed Banana War was an attempt by the Big Three, and Chiquita in particular, to get their hands on this lucrative business; to remove quota restrictions and reduce the tariffs they must pay, thereby cutting the price paid to ACP producers and putting them out of business.

In 1995 the brand-new World Trade Organization (WTO) began to implement the no-less Byzantine rules that emerged from the Uruguay Round of the General Agreement on Tariffs and Trade (GATT). The WTO is empowered not merely to oversee the new rules, but to enforce them. In principle these favor free trade, though in practice – and short of self-interest – no-one quite knows what this means. It wasn't hard, therefore, to suggest that the European banana regime conflicted with the rules of free trade.

However, the Banana War was not only about bananas. Much bigger fish were frying: the relative power of governments, nations, trading blocs and corporations; the structure, control and profitability of agriculture; the Common Agricultural Policy of the European Union; the fate of small-island economies; the booty of free trade. In the form of the Banana War the WTO was given its most high-profile trial to date as the Supreme Court of Globalization. If this meant anything other than the interests of corporate oligopolies like the Big Three, then the deliberations of the WTO had yet to suggest what it was.

Meanwhile, the lives of many thousands of banana growers in the South hung in the balance. They had been there before. In fact, they had rarely been anywhere else. What did they think? How did they feel about events that affected them directly, but over which they appeared to have no influence at all?

In mid-1999 I made a journey to find out, and I discovered something I would not otherwise have known. It became clear to me that the Banana War was being fought between two equally outdated protagonists. On the one hand, in the form of the European regime, the legacy of colonialism; on the other, in the form of the 'dollar' regime promoted by Chiquita and the US Government, plantation slavery and florid ecological insanity.

The fact that the rulings of the WTO had invariably

favored the latter over the former was regrettable and potentially catastrophic in its effects. But neither of these two relics had anything useful to say about the future, which they could not, I felt sure, conceivably survive.

So the question was, what would replace them?

By this time I'd seen enough of fair trade to know it could work. It would not be unreasonable to raise my

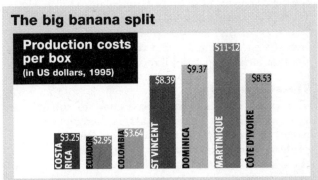

The big banana split

Production costs per box
(in US dollars, 1995)

COSTA RICA $3.25
ECUADOR $2.95
COLOMBIA $3.64
ST VINCENT $8.39
DOMINICA $9.37
MARTINIQUE $11-12
CÔTE D'IVOIRE $8.53

Banana Statistics, FAO, Rome, 1999.

The dollar banana of the Big Three is 'cheaper'. The real cost of a banana is not, however, quite what the price alone suggests. Ecuador has been in turmoil. Desperate for foreign currency to resolve a spiraling economic crisis, Ecuador has been flooding world markets with its bananas, causing the price to collapse and even the Big Three to feel the pinch.

Over half the production costs of a box of bananas are due to the hard labor involved. Wages in Ecuador or the Central American plantation economies are roughly half the incomes of small farmers in the Windward Islands, like Dominica or St Vincent – which are by no means princely themselves. Plantation economies flourish on what is, in effect, slave labor.

The plantation system uses large quantities of chemical poisons – more than ten times the average even for intensive agriculture in industrialized countries. Nematicides – to kill nematode worms – have sterilized tens of thousands of plantation workers.

Plantations also destroy the local environment; sophisticated drainage systems leach the nutrients from the soil and, in combination with other residues like copper, leave the land sterile. The fragility of the exposed soil and the concentrated flows of water cause severe soil erosion and increased flooding during tropical storms. Large quantities of fish, coral and animal life are lost to poisonous chemical agents. ■

sights a little and begin to tackle a larger, recurring theme – the connection, or lack of it, between fair and 'organic' trade, between equity and the environment. Would it be possible to discover what I had come to think of as the 'perfect' banana – one that was both fairly traded and organic?

To avoid undue disappointment, I began where I was unlikely to find it, in Guatemala. On its short Caribbean coastline, squashed between Honduras and Belize on a flat, swampy plain, the modern banana industry was invented – and the term 'banana republic' first took on its baleful meaning.

The search begins

The ticket collector was determined to squash the mosquito. He was chasing it across the cracked windshield of a hand-me-down American school bus as it rattled out of Puerto Barrios, the only sizable port in the region. Why did this look so odd? This was, after all, a tropical swamp, where you can expect to get eaten alive by mosquitoes and there's not much point in taking the trouble to kill a single one. Yet I hadn't been bitten once. And there were no birds. There was, I suddenly realized, little evidence of life of any kind.

Except, of course, for banana plants. Countless thousands of them. Mile upon endless mile, lining the roadside in numbered squares like the serried ranks of some godforsaken army decked out in uniform green headgear and ramrod trunks, holding out white plastic bags that flapped in the turgid breeze like banners draped over growing bunches of bananas.

This is the Guatemalan territory of Chiquita Brands, which is a direct descendant of the United Fruit Company. They used to call this company *el pulpo* (octopus) because its tentacles reached into every crevice of Guatemalan life. Established in 1899, United Fruit pioneered the plantation system of banana cultivation and by 1949 owned 3.5 million acres (1.4 million hectares) of Jamaica, Cuba, the Dominican Republic, Panama, Honduras, Nicaragua and Colombia. Its largest domain, however, was in Guatemala, where it owned Puerto Barrios as well as every mile of railroad in the country.

In 1954 United Fruit – guided by legendary PR man Edward Bernays – orchestrated US support for the overthrow of the elected government of Jacobo Arbenz, which intended to expropriate 400,000 acres (162,000 hectares) of its land and support the demands of banana workers for better pay and conditions. Violent repression ensued and has plagued the country ever since. Anxious to distance itself from accusations that United Fruit were dictating US foreign policy, the US Government eventually began a federal antitrust suit against United Fruit's banana monopoly, and in 1958 the company was broken up. Chiquita Brands, the Dole Food Company and Del Monte Fresh Produce, the 'Big Three' banana companies of today, are its offspring and you can still see the genetic resemblance in them all too clearly.

Union activist

Feliciano sat beside me on the bus. He was looking after me, though I was not entirely sure who was looking after him, an active trade unionist in a place where this is a dangerous thing to be. Gentle and attentive, he had agreed to show me something of what life is like on the banana plantations. His family had worked for bananas for 60 years: his father had 'retired' to a small-holding and absolute poverty some time previously, but he and all his brothers still worked on the plantations.

The bus slowed to a halt. A man in a sap-blotched vest, seated on what looked like a broomstick, hurtled out of the banana plants to one side of us, floated across the road in front and disappeared into the plants on the other side. The ticket collector, who had killed the mosquito, got off the bus and pushed back an overhead rail so that we could proceed. In due course we caught up with the man on the broomstick, punting rhythmically through the banana plants with two poles, flying along the cable-way that was made to carry off their fruit, into spotlights of burning sunlight, like Tinkerbell across a stage set for Peter Pan.

'Stop the bus! We're getting off!' cried Feliciano, some distance further on.

We stood in the dust left by the departing bus, in front of a large, dark barn of corrugated iron, its skirts lifted from the ground for ventilation. Inside there were empty concrete tanks, benches of steel rollers, industrial remains with mysterious functions. There was a wooden table, into which had been etched in ink the squares of a chess board. From here, Octaviano and Guillermo watched us guardedly as we approached.

'Welcome to Alabama/Arizona,' said Feliciano. 'The *finca* [literally 'farm', but better translated here as 'plantation'] that belongs to Victor Manuel Morales Hausseler. In theory, at least. Compañeros Octaviano and Guillermo will explain.'

Meeting the workers

'We are totally destitute,' said Octaviano. 'Totally destitute. We have nothing to eat or drink. They cut off the electricity and the water. We have to raise drinking water from wells. It is polluted. We're being poisoned.'

From the tremor in his voice I sensed the force of frustration in a story told too often to no effect. 'Well, we're just sitting here. Waiting. There used to be more than two hundred of us, men, women and children. But some have drifted away. There are about a hundred of us left. Like I said, we're just waiting.'

'For what?' I asked.

'For something to happen,' said Octaviano.

'It began with the women,' interrupted Guillermo, suddenly animated. 'The way they were treated. They were the ones working here in the packing plant. They had to use chemicals that made them sick, in the washing tanks, gave them sores on their feet. All times of the day, and late into the night too. Many of them are single mothers, and they weren't allowed to feed their children. Well, it got to the point where we weren't prepared to put up with it any more.'

'The only way to protect ourselves was with a union,' said Octaviano. 'There were lots of rumors flying around. The company was getting jumpy. Part of the plantation is on the other side of the river, and there's a bridge across it for the cableway, which we had to use to get to work. They came with armed guards and dogs to stop us crossing it, to split us up. So we were forced to use small boats. The river is very dangerous. Sometimes the guards would shoot into the water, trying to scare us. And then we were all sacked, with almost a week's wages still owing to us. The company has broken the labor laws of this country. The Government should be enforcing the law, but it doesn't. The courts are always on the side of the companies. We've been waiting to be reinstated ever since.'

'When did this happen?' I asked.

'February,' said Guillermo.

'Six months ago?' I asked with alarm.

'Eighteen months ago,' said Octaviano.

A few months after I left I heard that the Government had finally been persuaded to promote a settlement that recognized the union and reinstated at least some of the workers in their jobs – a small, if fragile victory achieved against apparently hopeless odds.

A few miles further down the road we entered a village where a thousand people lived – the families of the workers on Finca la Inca, at the end of the bus route and almost into Honduras. Stunted trees and mean little hutches lined the only street. As Feliciano and I strolled through the village we were followed by a man in uniform carrying a pump-action shotgun. Crawling behind him was a Pepsi delivery truck. It used to be raided by children under contract to Pepsi bootleggers. In Guatemala, value is signified by the size of the weapons touted around it.

We first saw Francisco sitting outside his house. He was on the executive of the Finca la Inca union, which was recognized by the company. Reluctantly and slowly, the Big Three had been accepting trade unions on some of the *fincas* they controlled. Feliciano believed that by improving international links between banana unions in the early 1990s the *Co-ordinadora de Sindicatos Bananeros de América Latina* (banana unions' federation), based in Costa Rica and Honduras, had had a marked impact. Guatemalan labor law, however, permits the formation of unions only in individual companies. So there were many small unions, one for every unionized *finca* of 200-or-so workers, and communication between them was extremely difficult.

Francisco, Feliciano and I sat down. There were only two chairs, so Francisco squeezed himself into his child's chair which cracked ominously under his weight. We were joined by Ubaldo, a powerfully built man just in from an eight-hour shift on the plantation. He was plainly exhausted, sinking into a tiny hammock strung between two trees. We talked about the difficulties they faced.

Wage freeze

Their wages averaged $0.63 an hour, $28 a week. Fixed almost three years previously, the rate was overdue for review. But the companies had made full use of Hurricane Mitch, the terrible storm that hung over the region for four days in October 1998. Though the devastation and death toll in Guatemala did not reach the same levels as in neighboring Honduras, still the rivers here had ripped away bridges and filled houses with silt, flooding banana plantations along their banks. The companies extended the wage agreement and sacked 'redundant' union members, claiming the damage done by Mitch as the reason.

At COBSA (a Guatemalan front company for Dole) they went one stage further. Members of the 'yellow' company union were induced to make legal complaints against the independent trade union, claiming its members were responsible for 'damages and prejudice' valued at $7.5 million in the wake of Mitch. Armed guards with dogs stripped the roofs off their houses to force

Free trade unions – a dark hard history

UN-sponsored Peace Accords were drawn up in Guatemala in 1997, formally bringing to an end 40 years of genocidal conflict which left hundreds of thousands dead and 45,000 'disappeared'. People expressed relief that the Accords had been agreed. But the underlying conflicts remained largely unresolved, and among these was the relentless persecution of the Guatemalan labor movement.

UNSITRAGUA, based in Guatemala City, represents some 74 member unions active across a wide range of employment, from the *maquila* export-processing factories to rural workers and banana plantations. It still has to operate semi-clandestinely, despite the Accords which give assurances on free trade unions, and UNSITRAGUA activists continue to feature on blacklists for arrest and assassination.

'We have a dark, hard history,' said Julio Coj of UNSITRAGUA. 'You could not speak or say what you felt and suffered, because you would be assassinated immediately. But we think that if we keep hiding our faces and our names, then we endorse the impunity that the Government and business sector still try to maintain.'

That much, he said, remained unchanged. 'We have peace on paper, but not a real and concrete peace. To make that we need full respect for union rights and for collective bargaining. The Government does not play its proper role, which is to balance business and union interests. There needs to be a radical change of attitude in business mentality and especially in the courts, which should uphold such meager protection as we get from our labor laws, in conformity with the conventions of the International Labor Organization. But they remain in the pocket of big business.'

'What matters for the workers is that the Government makes sure that all transnational companies respect the law. At the moment that's getting much more difficult, because globalization is allowing transnationals to produce what they like where they like, with no impediments. The tragedy is that this process is creating more, not less, poverty for us in Latin America.' ■

them to leave the *finca*. The courts duly issued *ordenes de captura* (arrest warrants) against 150 union members. Most were still in hiding, though among those arrested was a union official in Guatemala City. It said little for the case against him – or any of the others – that his passport proved he had been in Britain attending an international conference on poverty at the time the 'damage' was alleged to have been done in Guatemala.

Chemical cocktail

Along the roads were posted 'Notices to the Public' warning against entering the plantations while aerial fumigation was underway. The Big Three routinely claim that they do not fumigate when workers are in their plantations. Feliciano, Francisco and Ubaldo laughed heartily at the claim. If the workers got out every time fumigation took place, they said, there'd have been no bananas cut at all.

'It's not so bad in the mornings,' said Ubaldo. 'But, as the heat increases, these foul-smelling chemicals seem to rise up in the air, you have to inhale them and you begin to feel nauseous and have difficulty breathing.'

I asked what the chemicals were called. They had no idea. Francisco fetched a wad of blue plastic strips. These are sometimes placed around the stems of the bunches as a substitute for the intensely toxic concentrations in the plastic bags used to protect the growing fruit. He asked me to smell them. There was a deep foulness to the odor.

Feliciano had given me a copy of the *pacto collectivo*, the union agreement they had fought long and hard to achieve at the Pamaxan plantation, where he worked. On the face of it, this was a benign document granting the union formal recognition. But there were clauses regulating almost every aspect of their daily lives; not just working conditions and pay but schools, healthcare, water and electricity supplies, housing, transport, recreation facilities, books for the union library, football shirts, basketballs, toys for the children and even clocks.

At Finca la Inca I looked around me and asked if there was anything, besides the union, that wasn't controlled by the company.

'No,' said Francisco. 'Not apart from the Catholic Church over there.' He pointed to a wooden shed across the street. 'And the company refused to give them electricity. So they have to pray in the dark.'

Did he ever eat bananas?

'Good lord, no!' he said, looking genuinely surprised. 'People in places like this don't eat the fruit of their labor.'

I reflected to myself that although the offspring of the 'octopus' that was United Fruit had had, by 1999, precisely 100 years to establish their value to the local community, they had achieved nothing. From time to time they acted as if they didn't want to poison their employees or pay them shameful wages. But they were hooked. Always they had pulled back, resorted to crude coercion, because otherwise they were at risk of extinction. In truth, despite the outward appearance of a modern, efficient agricultural industry, they were an industrial dinosaur.

All the talk of *ordenes de captura* and guns and dogs and escape into hiding brought a single word to my mind, but I had refrained from using it because of the sensitivities involved. Ubaldo's great form, exhausted but relaxed now, swung in the tiny hammock. He looked into the distance in silence.

'It's just this wretched poverty,' he said eventually. 'We cannot get away from it. You know what it is?'

'You tell me,' I said.

'Slavery,' he said.

Exactly the word I'd had in mind.

Next stop: Dominica

I had taken a big step away from the perfect banana. So I flew off to the Windward Islands, across the Caribbean from Guatemala, to see if something closer to it could be found on the other side of the Banana War front line. I'd picked on the island of Dominica.

'We don't want to be in a market competing with producers like Chiquita,' said Gregory Shillingford emphatically, 'with a fruit that doesn't taste good, uses a lot of chemicals and employs slave labor. We do not want to endanger our environment. We want to promote reasonable wages for all working people, and a good relationship with consumers.'

Well, this made something of a refreshing change, and if any one person in Dominica could make this happen then I guess it had to be Gregory Shillingford. As General Manager of the Dominica Banana Marketing Corporation (DBMC) he was a key figure in the island's banana trade and carried a big responsibility on his broad shoulders. Dominicans rely very heavily on bananas, which account for some 20 per cent of Gross Domestic Product, 60 per cent of exports of goods, and the income of maybe 10,000 people – a very large chunk of the 90,000 population.

But bananas also delivered this tiny island's people into a fatal reliance on a single export crop that had also, inevitably, betrayed them. Production was in headlong decline. In the peak year of 1988, 72,000 tons of bananas were exported from 15,000 acres (6,075 hectares) of cultivation by 7,000 growers. But then falling prices, a spate of hurricanes, a tangled and more 'liberalized' single market in the European Union after 1992, all took their toll. In 1998 just 28,000 tons had been exported from 7,000 acres (2,835 hectares) by 2,800 growers – a reduction by more than a half. In villages around the island, stores that once sold basic necessities, most of them imported with banana money, had closed down.

Even so, preferential access to the European Union market continued. Between them, the Windward Islands still had an annual, duty-free quota of some

287,000 tons of bananas. Yet they sometimes use less than a half of it. Growers were evidently either unwilling or unable to produce more bananas. They were deserting the battlefront. If the European banana regime was such a good deal, why should this have been so?

Gregory Shillingford quoted a telling statistic: more than 80 per cent of the total crop in Dominica came from just 1,200 growers. The remaining 1,600 relied on the DBMC's obligation to buy their bananas. 'We don't really mind,' he said, a little halfheartedly. 'But what we need is growers who are business people, not peasants.'

Growers' gripes

Small farmers who own their own land are not, however, merely a quaint feature of Dominican society. They have shaped its history almost entirely, giving it an idiosyncratic, egalitarian, periodically febrile nature. No-one with any sense assumes that their interests can be taken lightly.

'Lots of small growers, particularly the older ones, are giving up their banana plots because it's all getting far too difficult, far too regimented,' said Irvince Auguiste as we pass a bedraggled collection of abandoned plants on a steep hillside. For ten years Irvince was the elected Chief – 'rather like being Mayor' he said – of the Carib Territory, through which we were driving. In 1902 some 3,000 acres (1,215 hectares) on the east coast of the island were handed back by the British to the few remaining descendants of the Carib peoples. Today, 3,700 of their heirs hold the same land in common, from which some 200 growers still produce bananas. They are a reminder that this is a special place.

'It used to be a much simpler thing,' continued Irvince. 'People would grow bananas and do other things as well. Now you have to keep diaries and charts and add up columns of figures and do exactly what you're told if you want to be a certified grower and get a decent price for your bananas. There's no time for anything else.

'Then you've got to be able to "bounce back" from hurricanes, which keep destroying your crop. Remember, small farmers have very little security. They can never be quite sure how good their crop will be, or when the next hurricane will strike, or even if there'll be a crop at all. It's not like having a regular wage and it's very easy to get into debt, because you have to invest in the crop before it is harvested. Sometimes they abandon bananas and then, when they find they can't earn a living from anything else, go back to them again. My father grew bananas, and I carried them on my head as a boy. But I don't grow them myself. Just recently, though, I've been having second thoughts...'

A big, red, battered pickup hurtled towards us round a hairpin bend. Irvince signaled to the driver, scarcely visible above the steering wheel, who screeched to a halt and wound down the window. She was slightly breathless. They chatted.

'Balene Fredrick,' said Irvince as she took off again. 'Just having a breather from the softball cricket match, to check on her kids. You know, she's one of our best banana growers. Let's go back and talk to her.' We set off in pursuit. She'd already disappeared round the next bend. 'What a woman!' said Irvince admiringly.

More means less

Balene and three of her kids were waiting for us in a roadside tin shed. Every small grower had a 'field' packing shed like hers. Handsome bunches of freshly cut bananas were laid out on tiered shelves, graded by size and labeled 'Geest'. To one side was a half-packed Geest box. In front of the bench was a large plastic bowl containing a washing solution. Chemicals were used here too, but much more sparingly than in Guatemala. Pinned to the back of the shed were complicated charts showing how the color-coded production cycle had to be followed. You could tell how she cared for her bananas from the way she handled them.

I asked her how much she earned from them each week. 'Just about enough to keep the children,' she said. 'What with their clothes and food and schooling, they cost a lot of money. In a way, I wish I didn't have to grow bananas. It never stops, and you have to do everything just right. It seems to get harder and harder, and we seem to earn less and less.'

The island is one of the most beautiful places I have ever seen. But it attracts few tourists. I fear that the two are related. There's no airport for wide-bodied jets, and therefore there are no golf courses, casinos or 'resort' hotels. White sandy beaches and blue lagoons are few and far between. Tentative steps were being taken towards eco-tourism, to complement Dominica's chosen image as 'The Nature Island'. A 'rainforest tramway' was being constructed 'for the less-athletic eco-tourist'.

There were firm plans, too, for an international airport. This would destroy homes, a school and scarce acres of relatively flat, productive agricultural land. It would plunge the people of Dominica deeply into debt, as well as the quagmire of graft that surrounds all such projects. Short of selling their land to hotels and golf courses, changing into flunky clothes and training to be servile, it was hard to see how mass tourism would benefit most Dominicans – or suit their disposition.

One possibility that had indeed been discussed, said Gregory Shillingford, was organic and fairly traded bananas. Some 15,000 acres (6,075 hectares) of banana land had lain fallow for at least five years (and were therefore free of chemicals), and the growers owned their own land, so the potential was there. So far, however, no-one had taken the plunge. Perhaps there was another future for this extraordinary place that had yet to be disentangled from its history.

Indeed, some time after I left, headway was made and the Windward Islands began to develop fairly traded and organic exports. The need for this became increasingly urgent as world banana prices collapsed. This simultaneously increased the interest in fair trade among desperate banana growers – and made the price of fair-trade bananas for consumers in the North seem that much higher by comparison. Fair trade in bananas faced its next severe test.

Dominican Republic

However, while I may have got closer to the perfect banana in Dominica than in Guatemala, I had not yet found it and still did not even know whether it existed at all. I set off for the Dominican Republic, my final destination, with no great expectations. The country is little more prosperous than Guatemala, and considerably less so than Dominica. Like Guatemala, it has suffered from the attentions of the United States, including an invasion by US marines. Bordered to the west by Haiti (one of the most poverty-stricken countries in the world) the Dominican Republic already is what Dominica threatens to become – a center for mass tourism. So I traveled to Ázua, close to the border with Haiti – and far from the cosmetics of tourism around the capital, Santo Domingo – feeling that my quest was probably futile.

And then I ran into an extraordinary story. It really began in 1992, with a small environmental disaster. In the mountains that march westwards across the troubled border with Haiti, there were 250 families living in a state of virtual destitution. They began to burn down the forest in which they lived, to make charcoal for sale.

'We didn't really want to do it,' said Angel Custodio, a shrewd, articulate man who was in the early years of an active retirement. 'The forest is a living thing, and we were killing it. We knew it couldn't last long. Our environment is alive, and we want to protect it. But we had no choice, no other way of making a living. So we asked the Government for help.'

They were lucky. The Government built an entire village for Angel's community, complete with utilities, paved roads, health center, school, church and halfway decent houses, on the coastal plain just outside the small town of Ázua. It also handed over to them a plot of fallow, fertile land large enough for every family to have its own 'parcel' of at least two hectares – sufficient to live from. So the erstwhile charcoal burners set to work growing maize, yucca, ground provisions – and a few bananas. They used no chemicals because, admitted Angel Custodio, they simply didn't have the money.

The people of Finca 6 would doubtless have remained in much the same situation had it not been for two further strokes of good fortune. Well, the first must be a mixed blessing. I have never been anywhere quite so hot. Even inside the cab of an air-conditioned pickup the thermometer registered well over 40 degrees centigrade. The heat is, however, relatively dry. That is bad news for plant diseases that need a good dose of humidity to flourish. But, with a high water table beneath them and good irrigation, it is very good news indeed for bananas.

Their second piece of good fortune was that, around the towns of Monte Cristi and Mao in the north of the country, two Dutch agencies were helping to develop fairer ways of producing bananas. Solidaridad and Max Havelaar (pioneers in the fair-trade coffee business) were making some headway across notoriously stony ground.

Savid to the rescue

So too was a young Dutch woman, Jetta van den Berg. In 1994 she set up a marketing company in Ázua she named Savid SA – an elision of *salud* ('health') and *vida* ('life'). Savid took on the tricky business of developing an unconventional product: organic bananas. It worked. The company helped to make the Dominican Republic the world's largest producer of organic bananas, with over 80 per cent of the total. Though accounting for just 27,000 tons in 1998, the world market for organic bananas was expanding fast, at an average 30 per cent per year, and demand consistently exceeded supply.

So Savid had to go looking for more producers and approached Finca 6. 'The market for organic bananas looked as if it was better than for our other produce,' said Angel, 'and so we began to develop our production for Savid. And now we do think, one hundred per cent, that organic production is better than conventional methods. I assure you, we're not just thinking about our own lives, our own health, but the lives and health of consumers as well, and about how to develop our own country – and why not others as well?'

Fresh approach

A severe test came in September 1998, when Hurricane George swept across the Dominican Republic and destroyed most of the country's banana crop, including that of Finca 6. In marked contrast with the way the Big Three exploited Mitch in Guatemala, Savid continued to finance the growers through to recovery, and they were now returning to full production, their confidence shaken but intact.

Porfirio Acosta Gil had a mobile phone that never stopped ringing. 'One request after another!' he sighed. 'I should turn the damn thing off.' He was the Production Manager for Savid, the head of a team of agronomists and evidently a revered figure.

All around us were flourishing banana plants that lived without chemicals of any kind. Porfirio assured me that it was real enough. Organic certification was by the German agency BCS, and tests were rigorous.

There was nothing very mysterious about it, he explained. The prime requirement is for meticulous tending of the plants, cutting away dying leaves, keeping the topsoil clean, removing the flowers from the bunches at the right time, covering them with reusable, chemical-free plastic bags to encourage growth and prevent damage from birds and surrounding leaves.

The same 'one follower' system is used here as elsewhere: successive shoots are named 'mother', 'daughter', 'granddaughter' and others are prevented from growing. Because of the aridity, the lower stem of the 'mother' is preserved after cutting, to allow its moisture to drain into the successor shoots. There are irrigation channels that use ground water pumped from wells. Spraying is with citrus oil which controls most, if not all, banana diseases. Organic fertilizer was imported from Costa Rica, though production was being developed here. We visited the plant, where large piles of animal droppings and compost attracted the most gigantic mosquitoes, and I was bitten at last.

Porfirio had the air of someone who knew his talents. I imagined that his skills could have commanded very much bigger rewards from straightforward commercial companies.

'You know, for all the bother of this job, I get tremendous satisfaction from it,' he said. 'It satisfies me, it really does, to be involved in something that people are committed to, with people who are overcoming their poverty, with building something good. At this moment, I wouldn't want to do anything else.'

Associated benefits

At first, the individual farmers of Finca 6 weren't so sure how to work. Jetta van den Berg and Savid were insistent that they should make up their minds: dealing with each one of them individually would be impossible. 'We thought about forming a cooperative,' said Angel. 'But, well, our experience of rural cooperatives hasn't always been very positive. Too much cheating, I'm afraid. So we decided to set up an Association.

Each of us still owns our "parcel", but we all belong to the Association, which meets regularly, elects officers to deal with Savid and things that affect us all. For example, if one *parcelero* doesn't tend the plants properly there's a risk of disease spreading to all of us.'

Angel took some satisfaction from the fact that neighboring growers wanted to join Finca 6. That, he believed, was a real measure of its success. The best advice he could give them was to form their own association, and Finca 6 would help them. 'We want people, especially poor people, to be united. If you have money, then you can live as you like. But if, like us, you don't, then sometimes you're going to need a service from somebody that isn't money, a service given individually, personally, between people. By being organized we can achieve this.'

And so, in 1997, Finca 6 was certified as a fair-trade producer by Max Havelaar. As we talked we sat beneath the roof of a new *comedor* (diner and meeting place) for the growers – one product of the fair-trade price premium they received. There were plans to build much-needed warehousing as well.

So Finca 6 had achieved something very, very rare: an organic and fairly traded product. I tried thinking of this extraordinary achievement as mere good fortune, unrepeatable elsewhere. But was it just a matter of luck that a government should justify its existence from time to time, and assist the people it claims to represent? Was it mere coincidence that, in the face of such a dreadful trade, people everywhere should defy bleak orthodoxy and search for something better? Was it pure chance that had given them the skill, imagination and commitment to make it happen? Of course not.

Fairly traded and organic

Fair trade can still apply, even where organic production is not possible. Organic production can still take place, even where fair trade hasn't yet been achieved.

Between them they could account for a much larger share of the banana business than they currently do. But it is only when they come together that organic production ceases to reflect the narrow self-interest of consumers, and fair trade fully respects the environment. Each complements the other.

Still, I had to have my doubts about Finca 6, if only because I knew what they were up against, and how far they still had to travel. For a start, the members of Finca 6 had turned over their plots almost completely to the production of bananas, creating dependency on a single export crop at the expense of their own food. Quite apart from hurricanes, the risks they faced were daunting. Organic methods are still not completely effective against some of the most virulent banana ailments, such as Black Saratoga and fungus. Then again, and sooner or later, the market for organic bananas would surely prove as treacherous as any other. Savid SA itself had just one shareholder: Jetta van den Berg. A great deal seemed to depend on her.

Working together

I walked with Porfirio through the parcel of Heriberto Custodio, who was the current President of the Association. My doubts began to fade into perspective. Just as I had been told they would, other *parceleros* arrived to give Heriberto a hand. They worked with their machetes in an easy rhythm, cutting back surplus shoots, cleaning the irrigation channels, lopping off unhealthy leaves, chatting and joking as they went. They did not have the driven, mechanical movements of rural laborers, though the work was no less strenuous in the tremendous heat. Porfirio looked around with sharp eyes, pointing from time to time to a leaf here that needed pruning, a flower there that needed plucking, the first evidence of leaf spot; coaxing, teaching, encouraging.

'These plants are so productive,' he said. 'You know,

they are just as productive as on the big plantations. Perhaps more so. All it takes is a little knowledge, care and skill. And a lot of hard work, of course.'

I asked him how much a *parcelero* could earn.

'I don't really know, and I don't ask. But I've been told it's about $1,000 a month, and can be as much as $2,000.'

We were invited to Heriberto's house. In the dining room a meal of fresh vegetables, rice and chicken was laid out for us. Heriberto gently complained about the unpaid labor he had to put in at the Association, the constant disputes he must resolve, the importance of what he had to do. But the trace of a smile never quite left his lips.

'You know,' I said to him. 'I don't think the banana workers in Guatemala would credit this... that there's a decent life to be had from growing bananas. You must be proud of what you have achieved.'

Fair-trade and organic bananas

The criteria for organic products are now firmly established and scientifically verifiable. For fair trade the situation is more complex. But, as for other fair-trade products, they include direct links between consumers and producers, a guaranteed minimum price and a price premium for producers, favorable financing and long-term commitments.

As yet, bananas represent only a tiny part of an organic market that in 1997 was estimated to be worth $10 billion worldwide. The European Union is the world's largest organic market, and Germany the largest consumer of organic bananas, with sales of over 6,000 tons in 1998. Britain is next, at about half that level. The US imports a similar quantity to Germany, and supplies the Canadian market.

The Dominican Republic is by far the largest producer, followed by Mexico. Japan imported 2,700 tons of organic bananas in 1997, mainly from the Philippines but also from Australia. Prospects for the market are thought to be extremely good, the main constraint being difficulties with supply. The price premium at retail level varies from 50 to 200 per cent.

Europe is also the largest market for fair-trade goods and in 1996 established the Fair Trade Labeling Organization International (FLO), an NGO which holds the register of certified producers across a growing range of products. The leading importer of fair-trade bananas is Agrofair, a joint venture formed by the Dutch NGO Solidaridad and producers in developing countries. Agrofair pioneered fair-trade bananas on the

'Oh yes we are,' cut in Heriberto's wife. 'You should have seen how we lived in the mountains, what this place was like when we first arrived. Now we can live with dignity. Here there is a future for our children.'

And then she brought in the bananas.

'You eat bananas?' I said

'Of course!' said Heriberto. 'They are very good for you, you know. Very nourishing. Very tasty. Don't you think it would be a little strange if we didn't eat them?'

'Very strange indeed,' I agreed.

I peeled back the skin, placed the naked fruit on my plate, cut a delicate slice, speared it with a fork and slipped it into my mouth.

'Well, what do you think?' asked Heriberto's wife.

'Delicious!' I said.

'Organic and fairly traded,' said Porfirio.

'Perfect,' I said. 'Quite perfect.'

Dutch market and accounts for more than 60 per cent of fair-trade banana imports into Europe. Their launch in the Netherlands in 1996 brought a market share of ten per cent within a few months and now averages five per cent – still the highest share for any fair-trade product in the country. The share in Switzerland remains at ten per cent. The price premium at retail level averages 20 per cent. Total imports into Western Europe rose from 12,500 tons in 1997 to 17,366 tons in 1998.

The main suppliers are farmers' cooperatives in Ecuador, the Dominican Republic and Costa Rica, as well as a farm in Ghana.

AlterTrade Japan has been importing fair-trade bananas from Negros in the Philippines since 1989. In Canada the Sustainable Development Institute and Oxfam Canada are looking to introduce the product into British Colombia under the Fair Fruit Initiative. Early in 2000, fair-trade bananas were launched in several supermarkets in Britain, and the initial results have been extremely encouraging.

Surveys suggest that 7.5 per cent of European consumers would buy fair-trade bananas at a price premium of 10 per cent, which translates into 300,000 tons a year. The need to buy import licenses as 'newcomers' under the European banana regime is the biggest constraint – in 1999 the allocation was limited to 276 tons per 'newcomer'. Large premiums therefore have to be paid to buy licenses from other holders, inflating the retail price to consumers and reducing payments to producers. ■

5 Blue jeans:
beaten by the brand

Would heaven have descended to earth if cars and computers were fairly traded too? A brief pause to consider whether the principles of fair trade can be made to apply more widely.

FAIR TRADE DOES work, at any rate for producers of tropical commodities like coffee, cocoa and bananas that cannot be grown in the North. The trouble is that unfair trade does not stop here. By far the largest part of international trade, in terms of money value at least, takes place not in commodities but in manufactured goods – the things that raw commodities are eventually made into. What about fair trade in computers, motorcars, garments?

The majority of the world's manufacturing labor force now works in the South, rather than in the North. Improved transport and communications have made it possible to manufacture things almost anywhere in the world. The South's 'comparative advantage' is in cheap labor, so it makes sense, on the face of it, to locate labor-intensive activity there. Export-processing factories have proliferated, and with them one of the defining features of globalization. Few motorcars, for example, are now made in any one country: the thousands of parts in the average family car come from literally dozens of different countries. Economic orthodoxy suggests that in this way wealth is rapidly reaching around the world as free trade spreads its wings.

There are, as you might imagine, flaws in this interpretation. The first is that free trade doesn't actually exist. There remain massive tariffs raised against those imports from the South that compete directly with 'value added' activities in the North. For example, a

tariff of 34 per cent is levied against processed chocolate (as opposed to cocoa beans) imported into the
European Union from countries like Ghana. Similar
tariffs and quotas are raised against textiles produced
in the South, under what's known as the Multifiber
Arrangement (MFA) that has survived in the new rules
of the World Trade Organization (WTO). The MFA is
particularly significant because textiles, which are
labor-intensive to produce, have traditionally been the
'first rung on the ladder' towards industrial prosperity
– most recently in places like Hong Kong and the
other 'export-led' economies of Southeast Asia.

The advocates of 'trade not aid' point out, with
some justification, that the South loses far more from
the tariffs imposed in the North than it gains from aid.
Truly free trade would therefore benefit the South.
What makes this argument difficult to counteract is
that the tariffs are purportedly imposed to save jobs in
the North, and so are frequently advocated by trade
unions, fearing a wages 'race to the bottom'. The mere
threat of 'relocation' to a cheap-labor country like
China exerts a very real downward pressure on wage
levels in the North – which is one reason why they have
stagnated or fallen, and the rich-poor divide has
grown even in rich countries like the United States.

Radical approach

Though calling for tariffs to save 'runaway' jobs in the
North may seem like the only practicable alternative,
in the longer term a much more radical approach
towards working conditions is required. This hinges
on the ability of the international labor movement to
organize around basic standards, such as those set out
by the International Labor Organization (ILO), which
the majority of the world's governments have
endorsed. This way, the movement has a common
project: the other way, national movements are at each
others' throats.

The family saloon car

A typical mass-produced small family saloon sold in, say, Denmark, will have been made in literally dozens of different countries, perhaps something like this:

BELGIUM
Tubes, seat pads, brakes, radio

CANADA
Glass, radio

NETHERLANDS
Tires, paints, final assembly

SWEDEN
Hose clamps, cylinder bolt, down pipes

SWITZERLAND
Underbody coating, speedometer

UNITED STATES
Valves, hydraulic tappet

MEXICO
Wheel nuts, lamps, steering wheel

SOUTH AFRICA
Clutch case, suspension brushes

MAURITIUS
Windscreen washer pump

INDIA
Carburettor, suspension brushes, steering shaft and joint

ITALY
Cylinder head, defroster grill

AUSTRIA
Radiator and heater hoses

DENMARK
Fan belt

NORWAY
Exhaust flanges

FRANCE
Alternator, master cylinder, clutch release bearings

INDONESIA
Seat stitching, hose clamps, switches, weatherstrips

JAPAN
Starter motor, alternator, cone and roller bearings, windscreen washer pump

SPAIN
Air filter, mirrors

BRAZIL
Oil pump, distributor, body panels

BRITAIN
Rocker arm, clutch, distributor, flywheel ring gear, heater, fuel tank, steering wheel

GERMANY
Locks, pistons, front disc, cylinder head gasket, battery

World Bank.

Secondly, transnational corporations control a much greater proportion of world trade (about two-thirds) than they do of more local 'domestic' trade. The growth of world trade strengthens their hand immeasurably. For this reason, if for no other, they have a vested interest in promoting it regardless of the consequences. The fact that the average breakfast, say, will have traveled some 5,000 miles (8,000 kilometers) to reach stomachs in the North, rather than jogged in from local food markets, is therefore a cause for celebration. If this means that hungry countries export food, so much the better. What would otherwise be patently insane suddenly seems to make sense.

So far, it is only fair-traders who have engaged in the detail of practical alternatives. The fact that they have been able to show what can be done, even in such a 'niche market' as Southern food commodities, naturally stimulates curiosity as to how the same principles might be applied more generally. What happens if we take a similar interest in something as iconic to contemporary consumer society in the North as, say, a pair of blue jeans?

Blue jeans

My love affair with blue jeans began when I got into a bath with my very first pair. In the days before pre-shrunk denim, this was what I thought you had to do with jeans labeled 'shrink-to-fit' – a fine early example of marketing spin.

There was about them a special aura. Hard to find in the shops, they could be repaired, embroidered, 'personalized'. You could stitch things on to them or cut them off. They were adaptable, from drainpipes to flares. You could make a statement without saying a word. They made you distinctive yet free from the fear of looking odd. In fact, in blue jeans you could be whatever you wanted: masculine, feminine, granny, groupie, peasant, potentate. Whoever you were, you could be someone else.

The original associations came, of course, from America via the Wild West and the Hollywood dream factory – youthful, individualistic, forward-looking. They were hard to resist if you were growing up as I was, in a war-weary, unctuous Britain still gazing backwards into the imperial sunset.

Icon status

Jeans fast went on to become an icon that clothed the universal promise of postwar consumer capitalism, insinuating the American Dream into the aspirations of anyone who could be persuaded to share it. Today you can find them down gold mines in South Africa, up mountains in the Peruvian Andes, from the forests of the Congo to the catwalks of New York and Paris. Eventually, when the flamboyant young designer of Paris haute couture, John Galliano, was asked on TV what he thought was the single most important garment of all time, you just knew he had to say 'jeans'.

I'm not sure when all this began to wear thin. Perhaps it was when sick 'poverty chic' and 'grunge' hit the fashion catwalks in the 1990s, followed by 'heroin chic' in New York, both clad in blue denim. Or maybe 'youth' figured out that if you aspire to be someone else for too long you become nobody at all and end up in uniform. And then, since all jeans are basically the same, paying double for the new breed of 'designer' labels is hardly so smart.

In any event, after a boom in the 1980s sparked by the global selling-fest of the Los Angeles Olympics, sales of blue jeans and the labeled footwear that went with them began to slow and then fall away.

One day a young woman from Guatemala came to see me. She described to me her daily life in a (South) Korean-owned *maquila* – export factory – stitching jackets for the American market. Driven on by shrieking supervisors, she said, she made so many jackets in a day, and for so little money, that I could scarcely believe her. She assured me this was better than having no job at all, but I was unable to imagine what could be worse. As she talked, so softly, she trembled almost imperceptibly. News had already reached home that she had been speaking out. There had been threats against her children. I must not print her name or take her photograph. All that remained with me were her words.

So I remembered what I should never have allowed myself to forget. The true nature of a thing is not to be found in its 'image'. It lies in the materials and the people who made it. The icons of consumer capitalism are made in secret: the raw materials plundered from behind the perimeter fences of private property; the 'goods' stitched together in 'postmodern' labor camps, anonymous sheds filled with human misery, scattered around the world along the meandering borderline between consumers and producers, profit and loss. The 'image' of consumer capitalism lies.

Cotton facts

Jeans are made from cotton, and cotton has spread like the fronds of Deadly Nightshade across five per cent of the earth's cultivable surface, invading fertile land in hungry communities, sucking them dry with irrigation, shrouding them in poison. Cotton uses higher volumes of more toxic pesticides than any other crop. A quarter of the world's pesticides are sprayed on it, causing a million cases of human poisoning every year. More than half the cotton growing in the US in genetically modified. To make the fabric, cotton is treated with another concoction of chemicals. The dyes are made from synthetic toxins. Most of the vast quantities of toxins released by the textiles industry into the air, soil and water derive from the dyeing process. Fragile parts of New Mexico have been destroyed by the extraction of pumice for 'stone washing' jeans.

Fabric is too floppy, the human body too irregular and the stitching too intricate to allow for much automation beyond the sewing machine and the individual operator – almost always a young woman – making one garment at a time. This is very laborious. So jeans are stitched together in hundreds upon thousands of 'sweatshops' that have sniffed out the lowest wages in the world in places like Guatemala, Bangladesh and the Philippines, or in the immigrant 'rag trade' areas of Los Angeles, New York, Toronto, Sydney and London.

As a stock item, jeans have fallen prey to the concentration of capital in the retail sector – that is, to an ever-smaller number of ever-larger retail 'chains' that sell most of the garments we wear. They dictate what gets made, and collect half the retail price of the garment for their pains. It is their business to promote the slightest modification in design as a significant shift in 'fashion' – and a good reason to buy yet another pair of jeans.

So now, in the 'postmodern' age, our largest and most useful industry, supplying a necessity little less basic than food, has headed off in a cloud of poison back to the dark, satanic mills of the 19th century. This we call 'development'.

The benefit of all this is said to be that consumer capitalism provides us with endless convenience and choice. From the $10 working pair of blue jeans to the upscale designer 'label' selling for $100 and more, there's a pair for everyone.

But suppose you want something quite elementary – a garment that isn't drenched in poison and sweat. With a straightforward commodity, like coffee, you can quite readily find fairly-traded brands. But applying similar principles of environmental sanity and social justice to the complexities of cotton cultivation, spinning, dyeing, weaving, cutting, stitching, the rag trade and the fashion business in general is quite another matter.

The first step on the ladder

The Newly Industrializing Countries (NICs) or 'Little Tigers' of Southeast Asia began by exporting textiles and clothing onto world markets from the 1950s and 1960s onwards. Even with penal tariffs imposed by the Multifiber Arrangement (MFA), they succeeded in undercutting textiles made in traditional centers like Britain, where the industry contracted with massive loss of jobs.

Textiles have historically been central to the whole process of industrial development. Partly this is because making fabrics is labor-intensive, partly because as a basic necessity there is always a strong local market for clothing, and partly because the technology required is not too sophisticated. Famously, even in the early 19th century, India still possessed a huge textiles industry, in many respects far superior to that in Britain. The Raj, however, put an end to this industry and substituted imports from Britain.

The pattern of exports from the NICs from the mid-1960s to the mid-1990s shows how they moved on and others took over. First exports from Hong Kong, Korea, Taiwan and Singapore rose sharply as a proportion of their total trade. Then they began to decline as more sophisticated industries (electronics and computers especially) took over. In their place, textile exports from Thailand and Indonesia rose sharply – though the Southeast Asian crash of 1997 leaves a question mark as to whether they will be able to follow the original NICs onto the 'next step on the ladder'.

This is the model for 'export-led growth' that the World Bank and International Monetary Fund claim to have been following around the world. What this model does not accommodate, however, is export growth led by primary commodities in the majority of the world's poorest countries – which hasn't prevented the model being promoted regardless. ■

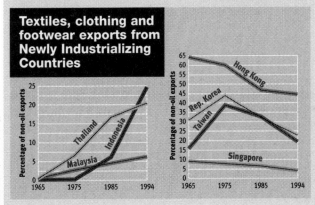

Textiles, clothing and footwear exports from Newly Industrializing Countries

Trade and Development Report, 1996, UNCTAD.

Blue jeans: beaten by the brand

The brand I began with, way back in the mid-1960s, was Levi's. Levi Strauss & Co – the world's largest garment company – has a benevolent reputation. It withdrew production contracts from Burma and China because of human-rights violations. When it discovered child labor at one of its contractors in Bangladesh it did not throw the children onto the streets, but offered education instead. It made great play of retaining garment factories with recognized trade unions in the US. It devised and implemented what was once widely regarded as a model corporate code of business ethics.

Relative to union-busting, sex-toting 'labels' like Guess? Inc – which in turn is more representative of the generality of labels – Levi's looks positively saintly, not to say smug. Perhaps it can afford to be so, charging as it does a healthy premium for the 'cult' status of its jeans.

Levi's in China

Still, Levi's is a long way from perfect. It has shown little serious interest in organic cotton and alternative fibers. It will not allow independent monitoring of its code, which makes it worth a great deal less. Then came massive job losses in the US – and a return to China.

Clarence Grebey of Levi Strauss, explained: 'It is a business decision based on our belief that we can now identify business partners in mainland China who will comply with our strict codes of conduct. If that's not the case, we will not do business there.'

Harry Wu, the US human-rights activist, responded: 'What's improved in China is the business climate. In fact, human-rights violations are getting worse. Forced labor is still used in the garment industry. There are no independent unions and anyone who tries to organize workers would end up in a re-education camp.' On balance, I feel more inclined to take the word of Harry Wu than Clarence Grebey.

So, between the big companies that dominate the jeans market, the choice is entirely relative. Among the worst is Guess? Inc. Because US garment workers, and their union UNITE, have promoted a boycott of Guess products, no-one in their right mind would touch them. Among the best, even now, is Levi's. But globalized 'cheap' labor and industrial cotton are integral to all of them. Corporate codes of conduct have their limitations. Business is business.

So I turned to the ecological front – studiously ignored by the big companies – where, to begin with, things looked a little more encouraging. The Internet threw up several suppliers of organic-cotton jeans, but they were sold only in North America. Panda, the catalogue of World Wide Fund for Nature (WWF), Zurich, offered 'Bio-Damensjeans "Girls' Fit"'.

I had also heard rumors that the original jeans were made from hemp, a fiber more usually associated with rope and sacks. There is a dedicated band of devotees who claim that hemp doesn't need pesticides and has 25,000 different uses: the war on drugs (yes, hemp is the source of marijuana) might be a scam by vested cotton interests to scupper a dangerous rival. Then the Body Shop launched a new line in hemp cosmetics – immediately condemned and therefore promoted by the drugs warriors – which made it feel like safer territory for me.

Hemp jeans

On the Internet again I found hemp jeans from Romania priced at $60 – but, once more, available only in the US. In a catalogue there was a pair priced at $150 – too extravagant for me. I set an upper limit for myself of $100 – steep enough, but at least in the same bracket as 'designer' labels. Then, through *Ethical Consumer* magazine, I found the Hemp Union of Hull, and Dick Bye on the other end of the phone.

Yes, he said, Hemp Union sold blue jeans at $100.

In fact, he sent me a pair in 'natural' color. They are lovely – softer and floppier than denim, like linen but tougher, warmer. There are very fetching, distinctive green leaves on the label, which says: 'If you try to smoke the garment you will get nothing but an awful headache. Save the Planet!'

What about the claim that Hemp Union products were 'manufactured without exploitation'? Well, he said, the jeans were made for a company in Denmark by a manufacturer in – China. The PC pair was, said Dick Bye, perfectly feasible, but would cost more than three times as much, 'and we don't feel that the current market would stand this'. I'm sure he was right.

Who pays the price?

I thought about this for a minute. If poison- and sweat-free jeans cost $300, who pays for the $50 pair? Why, the human environment and those young women in sweatshops, of course. In effect, they provide a subsidy to consumers. Think about this a little more, and you realize that if producers were paid more, so that they themselves could afford to buy fairly traded products that in turn cost less, and you'd be arriving at the right destination – and traveling in almost precisely the opposite direction to current orthodoxy.

The fact is, however, that the perfectly PC pair of jeans does not exist. We don't have that limitless choice after all. It is not just the image, but the promise, of consumer capitalism that lies.

As 'consumers' we do indeed have power. We should use it as constructively as we can, opting for the relatively good rather than the absolutely bad products. This means thinking differently, reclaiming the substance of 'identity' from the silly labels that litter the marketplace, deriving some sense of discovery – rather than inconvenience – from the process. Of course, in the rich world at least, 'consumer' movements have been active for some time. So far as jeans are concerned they have yet to make much difference, though perhaps we should not be surprised. After all, no-one ever changed anything of importance just by buying something else – but we can make a difference by not buying, and protesting, as consumer groups in the South have shown.

Meanwhile, the people who make jeans are busy figuring out how best to put things right. Eventually they must succeed, if only because humanity will not tolerate such shameful treatment for ever. So too, and thanks to a small but growing band of pioneers, organic cotton and alternative fibers are within reach of offering a viable alternative to industrial cotton. In the end they, too, must succeed, because the earth will not tolerate such mistreatment indefinitely, either.

If we wait until the globalizers have run out of runway, however, a wreck is all we'll find at the end of it. A political response, and political support for the alternatives, is now required. That means weaving the two strands of ecology and social justice together. All too often they run in parallel, preoccupied by their own priorities. Each tends to look on the other as an extra burden, a different history. But when they are woven together then each will be made stronger by the other, and change will at last be possible.

In the meantime, what we do have is a sense of direction. Truth to tell, it's a much more attractive, far less suicidal route than the one we're traveling now. It's been mapped out for us by people who refuse to accept that nothing can be done and no-one is listening. All we have to do is prove that they're right.

6 Buying it: fair trade in the North

A journey through the world of chocolateers and chocoholics with a Ghanaian cocoa farmer.

EVENTUALLY, FAIR TRADE reaches its final destination – the consuming societies of the North. It is here that, on average, 90 per cent or more of its value stays. There's a limit to what fair trade can do about this. So great is the dominance of an ever-smaller number of ever-larger retail chains that fair trade can't hope to reach the majority of people in any other way than from their shelves. It isn't yet big enough to sustain its own processing industries – ripening bananas, roasting coffee, grinding cocoa – and so has to rely on finding the few independent companies that are willing to do this for it, which doesn't come cheap.

Short of fair trade getting very much bigger it's not easy to see a way out of this. One of the great assets of Alternative Trading Organizations (ATOs) is that they do indeed create different retail systems – charity shops or 'direct selling' networks like Traidcraft in Britain or Equal Exchange in the US. If farmers' markets and neighborhood retailing initiatives can keep a foot in the door, then they – like the cooperative wholesale societies – do provide a sizable addition. But for the time being, if fair trade is to be a reliable option for a significant number of producers, there is no alternative but to fight for its space on supermarket shelves, where volume is the better part of value. Generating that volume, in turn, means resorting to marketing campaigns and 'brand awareness'. Before you know it – and if you're not very careful indeed – fair trade takes on an uncomfortably close resemblance to any other trade.

Well, fair-traders are used to getting their hands dirty and still keeping clean. In some ways their 'entryism' is more subversive than staying forever on the outside looking in. The risks involved are enormous, and doubtless there will be casualties that simply sink back into the mainstream. But there is one thing that makes this less likely, and that is the direct, personal links fair-traders have with producers. Try following the fair-trade path with them, rather than with their products, and the difference is clear from the start.

'What is a cocoa farmer who has never been out of his country before doing coming to the United Kingdom?' On the surface of it, a reasonable enough question. It was the imperious manner of the immigration officer that gave it its intimidating weight. Koto Asamoah Serebour stood looking very small and uncertain in his only good suit. A cocoa farmer, he had showed me what cocoa means to many Ghanaians. Now it was time to return the hospitality and show him the chocolate-consuming business in Britain. It was six in the morning at London's Gatwick Airport. No-one was in a good mood.

The first barrier

I went back to see if I could help. The immigration officer was incredulous. 'What is a Canadian (he said the word like it was some kind of social disease) doing trying to get a cocoa farmer into the United Kingdom?' I had naively assumed that once we had won the battle with the British High Commission in Accra it would be plain sailing. But Asamoah had at first been refused his visa and those clever devils at the High Commission had stamped the refusal right in his passport. At six in the morning at Gatwick Airport that was like a red flag to a bull.

Pretty tame stuff, compared to what many people have to put up with crossing borders, but the Athenian disdain of the voice of authority was still irksome. It was not just a question of Asamoah's skin color but also of his style. He lacked the self-assurance of the globalized robots who run the world economy and pass through immigration like a subway turnstile. Authority smells a lack of confidence like a Rottweiler smells fear.

Eventually the fact that Asamoah already had his visa got us through. But it was plain that this was an unusual and unwelcome state of affairs. It was okay for Asamoah's cocoa beans to travel to Britain, but he was expected to stay at home. It is one of the central ironies of the global economy – freedom for commodities and capital but not for people.

The idea was that we would try and get a look at various aspects of chocolate production and consumption. We had been warned that this would not be that easy, as big chocolate manufacturers are notoriously secretive about letting people tour their facilities. Our first refusal came from the good folks at Mars, who didn't want Asamoah to see how they made Mars Bars in Slough. Similarly, Cadbury's expressed skepticism when we approached them – even their trade union was reluctant to let us meet members to compare working lives in factories with those in the field. Undaunted, we pressed on.

Fair-traders

We went to London to meet the people at Twin Trading, the organization that supports small-scale farmers' access to markets. Here we got a good overview of what is being done by way of fair trade, as well as information about the cocoa trade and the politics and economics of Big Chocolate. The 'chocolate man' at Twin Trading was Simon Wright, who had become disillusioned working in the mainstream chocolate industry, where he was employed trying to reduce the already small amount of cocoa solids in the commercial British product. He now split his time between Twin and Green and Black's, who sell organic as well as the fair-trade Maya Gold chocolate bars. Simon traced for Asamoah the route that cocoa takes to get to market. All of it passes through the Dutch port of Rotterdam and then is processed by Dutch Cocoa into either cocoa liquor, butter or powder. It then becomes the key ingredient for chocolate manufactured in several locations in continental Europe. The fair-trade chocolate is made in either Switzerland or Germany with the cocoa butter being used by the Body Shop as a base for cosmetics.

Probably not very much of Ghana's cocoa ever made it into the huge British chocolate market. The best cocoa fetches a premium price that only high-grade chocolate manufacturers are willing to pay. Most British factories are not even set up to make high-grade chocolate. The opinion at Twin was that not much in the way of high-quality chocolate gets produced anywhere in the English-speaking world. Big Chocolate, which dominates the English (Cadburys, Mars and Nestlé) and the US (Hershey, Kraft, Mars and Nestlé again) markets, is more interested in a low-cost product than in high-quality chocolate with lots of cocoa solids. The average content of the leading market products is in the 20-per-cent range, whereas good European chocolate comes in closer to 40 or 50 per cent.

A rough, back-of-the-envelope calculation, based on a cocoa price of about $1,750 a ton, revealed that on a market-leading chocolate bar that sells at about $1.80 in the shops, a cocoa producer could expect to see about three cents.

Good chocolate

'Historically, the English have not wanted their chocolate to taste much like chocolate,' said Simon. 'Indeed, they haven't gone for any strong flavors at all. When you bite into most English commercial chocolate, the first sensation is a sweetish toffee kind of taste.'

But the interest in quality and safe food that is sweeping the Anglo-Saxon world may mean a brighter future for good chocolate. For fair trade the best option may lie in producing high-quality chocolate that uses lots of cocoa (with no chemical inputs) and returns a decent price to the farmer. This would allow the product to be marketed with an appeal to quality and health as well as fairness. Twin's big success story had been Cafédirect, their widely distributed ground coffee. The launch of Divine in 1998 added a strong, popular-tasting brand to the main fair-traded chocolate brands marketed on the continent, where fair-trade cocoa volumes are rising.

By and large, fair-traded chocolate has been slower to get off the ground than coffee. It proved hard to break the stranglehold of Big Chocolate, who are able to keep the price low and saturate the media with brand-identification advertising. If you want to do it differently everything costs more – more for raw materials, smaller more expensive batch runs in smaller factories. However, the chocolate market is so large and lucrative that even a very small market niche could mean a lot of money and a lot of cocoa. The arrival of Divine and, in 2000, of Dubble (for children) is taking fair trade to the corner shop, the gas station and the cinema for the first time, backed by an educational link to Comic Relief and teachers.

Speculative purchase

Our next stop after Twin was the trading floor of the London Futures Market (LIIF). Here Asamoah was very surprised that in the place devoted to buying and selling cocoa there was not a bean in sight. The level of abstraction involved with futures trading was hard for either of us to grasp. The scene was like something out of the film *Wall Street*. But the screaming and wild gesticulating of the traders in the pit seemed to Asamoah to be little more than 'a group of madmen' whose purpose was mysterious and obscure.

Our guides were at great pains to explain to us the underlying rationality of the trading system, despite its complexity. They pointed out that, unlike the New York futures market where there is much more pure speculation, 70 to 80 per cent of the buying and selling in London is based on 'physicals'. By this we took them to mean that contracts for the delivery of cocoa are mostly done by people in the industry (shippers, big trading houses, processors or manufacturers) with only 20 to 30 per cent done by those who have absolutely nothing to do with cocoa – the pure speculators. The big chocolate companies are mostly represented by stand-in buyers so that their ultimate 'demand' intentions remain disguised. The purpose of the market for those in the industry is to 'lock in' prices as a hedge against unexpected increases. This is understandable enough in a volatile market, where prices have been known to be as high as $4,800 a ton, and as low as $800.

Yo-yo prices

So far, so good. But only two to three per cent of these futures contracts at the exchange ever end up in the physical delivery of cocoa. Indeed, seven or eight times (even higher in New York) more cocoa is bought and sold on the exchange than exists or ever will exist in the world. Contracts are being bought and sold nearly two years in advance. This sounded to me like speculation, no matter who was doing it.

While these markets play a crucial role in setting the world price and what the farmer ends up getting, most actual deals for the physical delivery of beans are done by fax or over the telephone between the different players in the industry, by-passing the exchange entirely. Yet the exchange remains crucial in setting the price. A lot of people do very well indeed out of the futures market. One must be forgiven for the fleeting idea that this speculation is being done on the backs of hard-pressed producers who actually grow the beans, without whom this whole edifice would crumble. If there is this much money to be made in cocoa, why should it be so hard for Asamoah to get enough from his crop to pay the school fees for his youngest son in

The cocoa chain

A chocolate bar may look like a fairly simple thing to you. But, even after the bean has been grown, dried and dispatched from producers' countries like Ghana, it still has an extremely complex process to go through before it becomes a bar of chocolate – and then it has to be wrapped and distributed to retail outlets like supermarkets. These are the links between cocoa and chocolate, including the main corporations involved at the beginning – and the end of the chain. ■

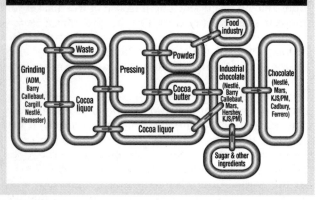

The links that bind cocoa to chocolate

Food industry

Waste

Powder

Grinding (ADM, Barry Callebaut, Cargill, Nestlé, Hamester)

Pressing

Cocoa liquor

Cocoa butter

Industrial chocolate (Nestlé, Barry Callebaut, Mars, Hershey, KJS/PM)

Chocolate (Nestlé, Mars, KJS/PM, Cadbury, Ferrero)

Cocoa liquor

Sugar & other ingredients

Cocoa Newsletter, No7.

Kumasi? Of course more sane ways of balancing supply and demand are not popular in this market-mad era with its demands to 'liberalize' everything.

Craig Sams' Whole Earth Foods produces Green and Black's organic chocolate. Fair-trade Maya Gold is made with cocoa from a cooperative in Belize. Sams has a broad vision of the political economy of food and a special interest in cocoa and chocolate. He saw the richness, flavor and individuality of good chocolate as tied to the unique care small farmers give to the variety of their trees and beans. He was certain this would never be replicated in the uniformity of plantation agriculture: 'Nothing in the world has such a complexity of flavors. There are over 400 distinct smells that come from the cocoa bean – the rose has only 14 and the onion just 6 or 7.' Sams found it distressing that cocoa is the world's most heavily sprayed food crop.

But he believed that the small farmer is ultimately the most efficient producer of beans. 'Plantations can only compete if they are run under conditions of slave labor, with extremely low wages – and people will only put up with that for so long.' The dramatic drop in the share of cocoa production from Brazilian and Malaysian plantations supported Sams' argument. An epidemic of Witches Broom disease on Brazilian plantations had shown the way genetic uniformity undermines agro-chemical crops.

Small means efficient

But if small is an advantage in cocoa production, it is not so in chocolate retailing. Sams had a hard time breaking into the huge British chocolate market. A combination of saturation advertising, clout with buyers and cheap production makes Big Chocolate a fierce competitor. Nonetheless, Green and Black's sales had been growing by 20 to 30 per cent a year.

Asamoah was quick to see the sales opportunity and asked if Sams had any place for his own beans from the Kuapa cooperative in Ghana. Sams was sympathetic, but would require them to be certified organic. Asamoah pondered the possibility. Later, as we toured some organic shops in London's West End, he became increasingly intrigued by the idea of Kuapa 'going organic'. He, like so many other Ghanaian farmers, had already cut down on chemical pesticides because of the expense. It might be difficult to convince other Kuapa members to cut out the cheaper, less toxic fungicides used against the devastating Black Pod disease. But Asamoah was beginning to think this could be the wave of the future: 'I think that everything that we sell should be organic. Otherwise we will be left behind and not able to sell our cocoa.'

We ended our tour in the Big Chocolate game.

Most chocolate companies – most food companies, for that matter – do not like groups of nosy customers wandering around their factories. So they have set up theme parks outside. The parks combine elements of the production process with a magical world where fantasy and history intersect in one glorious burst of self-promotion. We entered 'Cadbury World'.

The overwhelming impression was of sheer scale: one 12-hour shift packs 345,000 bars; 800 bars a minute; 12,000 tons a week. Despite chocolate's reputation as a luxurious food, for Big Chocolate it is, first and foremost, an industrial product. Although many of the operations in Cadbury World were still done by hand, in the real plant everything is automated. The idea is to give the customer the sense that Big Chocolate still regards chocolate-making as a craft, carried out under the 'watchful eyes of our most experienced chocolateers', who never tire of the stuff: 'They are chocoholics. Chocolate is a way of life.' Asamoah felt he'd rather work under his trees than on the line for Cadbury. He introduced himself to one younger worker and asked about the use of Ghanaian cocoa. The worker said that he thought most of the cocoa came from Malaysia.

Cadbury World takes the customer through a sanitized history of cocoa – no slaves here – to a 'craft-like' sample of chocolate-making, then a revealing survey of advertising around the world and over the decades. It all ends with a Disneyesque fantasy ride in little cars through a place called Beanville, where one meets such characters as the Bean Team and Mister Chunky Choc. The iconography is perfect – industry prying loose Third World raw materials, slapping them on the assembly line and then convincing the gullible that their purchase is a magic route to a fantasy happiness. In Spain the ads are set to flamenco guitar; in the US it is cutesy mini-egg bunnies.

For Asamoah, amazement was clearly the main

reaction. It was a long way down the cocoa chain from his eight acres in Ghana. The concerns of Big Chocolate to cut costs while increasing market share were a universe away from the struggle of West African farmers for a minimal well-being based on a decent price for their beans.

Big eats little

For the past few decades, most of the many chocolate 'brands' we recognize in the shops have been swallowed up by the major corporations – though you wouldn't necessarily know it by looking at the wrappers. Here are the little fish that have been eaten by the big fish. ■

PHILIP MORRIS/ KLAUS JACOBS SUCHARD
FreiaMarabou (Holland)
Côte d'Or (Belgium)
Terry's (Britain)
Csmege (Hong Kong)
Lacta (Brazil)
Olza (Poland)
Kuanas (Lithuania)
Republica (Bulgaria)
Poliana Zah (Romania)
Figaro (Slovakia)

NESTLÉ
Curtiss Brands (US)
Buitoni Perugina (Italy)
Rowntree (Britain)
Intercsokolade (Holland)
Perrier (France)
D'Onofrio (Peru)
Cokoladovny (Czech Rep.)
Goplana (Poland)
Maltschika (Bulgaria)

CADBURY SCHWEPPES
Piasten (Germany)
Productos Santi (Argentina)
Hueso (Spain)
Bouquet d'Or (France)
Neilson (Canada)

HERSHEY
Guber Schokoladen (Germany)
Poulain (France)
Sperlari (Italy)

But there are markets and markets. In the vast Kumasi market in Ghana, where Asamoah's daughter Gloria sells her tomatoes and onions, you can buy almost anything, but no chocolate or even cocoa beans. These markets are quite different from the long-distance export markets that trade cocoa before the pods even sprout from the trees. A drought may shift prices dramatically, but ultimately it is the projections of demand and supply by Big Chocolate, using all the paraphernalia of modern research technology and commercial calculations, that decide price. It's a contest of unequals, with the end buyer and seller barely even aware of each other's existence. The dif-

Unequal exchange

A recurrent theme in the 'commercialization' of all Southern commodities in the North is the way it is controlled by a very small number of very large transnational corporations. Add to this the growing power of the big retail chains – like Wal-Mart – and you begin to understand the near-monopoly or 'oligopoly' with which corporations ensure that the system operates in their interests. So long as they control one end of the trade – increasingly the 'consumer' end – then they can be pretty sure of deciding what goes on at the other, 'producer', end as well. The notion that world trade promotes ruthless competition is pure fiction. Corporations share more common interests than they have bones of contention.

So we can find very similar patterns of control across a range of commodities, from coffee to chocolate and bananas. A relatively new pattern is, however, also beginning to emerge. The risks associated with actual production are large, and the rewards are not very great. In this way the big corporations have been shifting their control away from production, which they are increasingly content to leave to small or 'independent' producers. In the end, these producers will, nonetheless, have to sell to the corporations anyway, and it is here, in the commercialization

Concentration of control

Coffee (market share, Britain)

Supermarket 'own labels' 14.8%

Other brands 6.5%

Kraft General Foods 20.8%

Nestlé 57.9%

Coffee Matters, Nestlé UK, 1993.

ference in life-experience between a dealer on the New York Commodity Exchange with a six-figure salary, and someone who owns a small cocoa farm in West Africa, is too vast to contemplate. Yet gaining competitive position for one may put the very survival of the other into question.

African markets are not like this. Here people look each other in the eye, discuss the quality of the goods, what is fair and what each party can afford. If the product doesn't meet expectations the buyer can return to complain directly. If the seller thinks the price offered is just too low there are usually other customers willing to pay a reasonable price. Prices more or less fit the

and 'branding' of products, that they now concentrate their efforts.

The pattern varies slightly from one product to the next. Bananas arrive in refrigerated 'reefer' ships and, short of being ripened for sale, require very little attention; they receive their corporate 'brand' directly on the skin. Coffee requires a little more processing through roasting and blending (and freeze-drying for 'instant' coffee), so the brand goes onto the jar, and this is where corporate power kicks in. Chocolate is more complex, requiring other ingredients (sugar, milk, fats) and frequently is further manufactured into heavily-promoted bars, biscuits and candies.

At one crucial stage or another, however, big corporations intervene in every product before it eventually reaches the final consumer. ■

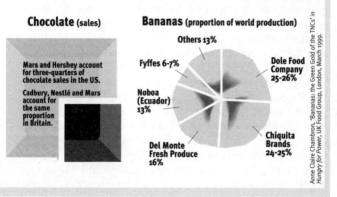

Fair Trade Yearbook, 1994 and Cocoa Newsletter, No3.

Chocolate (sales)

Mars and Hershey account for three-quarters of chocolate sales in the US.

Cadbury, Nestlé and Mars account for the same proportion in Britain.

Bananas (proportion of world production)

Others 13%

Fyffes 6-7%

Noboa (Ecuador) 13%

Del Monte Fresh Produce 16%

Dole Food Company 25-26%

Chiquita Brands 24-25%

Anne Claire Chambron, 'Bananas: the Green Gold of the TNCs' in *Hungry for Power*, UK Food Group, London, March 1999.

needs of human survival. There is an honesty and an equality here. So when next you hear the 'free market' being lionized, make sure to inquire which market the speaker has in mind.

Boosting fair trade

Serious efforts are being made to introduce fairness into international trade. These are closely tied to the production of high-quality chocolate. Farmers' co-ops like Kuapa, fair-traders like Twin Trading and fair-trade producers like Green and Black's, Divine and a number of others – mostly in continental Europe – are leading the way. In Canada and the US you can get Masaco chocolate from Bolivian cocoa; in Australia it's Force 10 from Samoan cocoa, and Trade Aid chocolate in Aotearoa/New Zealand. But a better price for cocoa remains far down the priority list of Big Chocolate, where trends are the same as those throughout the global corporate economy: merger mania, restructuring to reduce costs, and the battle for market share, mostly through heavily advertised, low-cocoa-content chocolate bars and candies.

Building an alternative unites the battle for fairness with that for a quality – often more healthy and organic – product. As Craig Sams from Green and Black's pointed out, it doesn't take much of a price-break to improve things for the small farmer: 'We screw people to the wall for so little. By giving a 25-per-cent premium to growers, Green and Black's add only four per cent to the cost of each bar, but for farmers that makes a huge difference.'

One way of giving a leg-up to fair-trade goods would be by reducing the sales tax on them. But in an era that glorifies the unfettered market this is bound to be greeted with screams of 'unfair subsidy'. Yet, for example, agricultural subsidies in Europe are estimated to add nearly $36 to the average family food bill every week. And, in the era of supposed free trade, Ghana's excellent chocolate would meet a 34-per-cent tariff if it ever reached a European port.

Things may not be all bleak for small producers. There is an emerging consensus that the small farm is the best way to produce cocoa as well as to preserve biodiversity. But all is not rosy for them either. The shifting pattern of production in Ghana has moved from east to west as soil fertility declines and trees age. Even small farmers face problems unless the best of grassroots science – integrated pest management, new ideas in inter-cropping, soil science – is made available to them. Who will be there to do this if structural-adjustment policies cut agricultural-outreach services to the bone, as they have done in Ghana?

If small farmers are to be the wave of the future they must do better out of a chocolate bar. Big Chocolate won't jump on its own – pressure is needed. On the political side, some of this is beginning to come from the 'Cocoa Platforms': alliances of unions, producers, fair-traders, environmentalists and other activists in the industry in Europe, Brazil and Ghana.

Economic pressure must also come from those who produce a higher-quality, cocoa-intensive product. If dissatisfaction grows with the cocoa-poor, sugar-heavy candy that Big Chocolate passes off on a public unaware of the alternatives, the market niche for better-quality chocolate will expand. Meanwhile – particularly for children, who do not like 'dark' chocolate at all – the arrival of boisterous fair-trade alternatives in mass markets ensures they aren't confined entirely to a 'niche'. Even a small drop in market share is something big companies cannot afford to ignore. So, as the political hucksters are fond of saying, this is a 'win-win scenario': good for farmers, good for consumers, good for the ecosystem. Don't feel guilty – buy fair trade and have another bite.

Conclusion: an infant among giants

Why free trade has no future but fair trade does.

WHEN WE PROCESS down the cathedral aisles of supermarkets we are participants in a form of cult ritual. Stacked on the altar shelves are thousands of branded icons intended to induce in us the impulse to buy. Anything close to the truth about how, where, by whom and with what consequences the icons were made is kept out of sight – a 'commercial secret' – because it could incline us to think twice and prove fatal to our faith. Our selection is passed across an electronic eye that computes the tribute we must pay. Finally, we head for home and consume our chosen icons.

From time to time we might recognize a familiar face behind the checkout till – a school friend perhaps, the child or parent of someone we know. This person may have learned from hard experience that the average consumer in full flow does not always make a very pretty sight – magisterial, forever on the verge of retail rage. Our friend at the checkout, as the only available face, is frequently on the receiving end of it and expected to be servile. Living at ease with consumer capitalism requires of us a facility for extreme behavior: compliant as producers, overbearing as consumers.

Economic orthodoxy makes great play of its ability to divide the world very neatly in two; credit and debit, asset and liability, profit and loss, supply and demand, producer and consumer. It argues that the two halves tend towards some kind of balance or 'equilibrium', though this it cannot actually prove from the historical record. In practice consumer capitalism always heads for the nearest crisis, veering wildly towards slump or boom, depression or elation as the mood takes it –

characteristics that in people would be symptomatic of a manic form of mental illness.

Caught in the untidy ambiguities of daily life, real people are neither consumers nor producers, never entirely one thing nor the other, always both at the same time. Without producers there would, after all, be nothing to consume – and no-one to consume it. Besides, there is a 'No Entry' sign posted outside those supermarket cathedrals for anyone who has not paid the price of admission by submitting to the tyranny of gainful employment. So what is a 'consumer' society supposed to be? If consumers are sovereign, over whom, precisely, do they exercise their sovereignty?

Confronting the free market

The last time people confronted rampant free-market world capitalism, in the 19th century – leading eventually to utter chaos and the industrialized bloodshed of two world wars – other options were quickly established. Workers' collectives, cooperative retail outlets, credit unions, mutual insurance and mortgage funds, all manner of ingenious alternative schemes proliferated. Savings and Loans institutions in the US, building societies in Britain, wholesale, retail and producer cooperatives around the world, were less an expression of idealism or political ambition than of practical necessity. 'Free' markets simply didn't supply food at prices people could afford; the relatively poor couldn't get access to credit; even funerals were beyond the reach of many. Mutual and cooperative alternatives became, in some cases, so effective at meeting these needs that people began to lose any sense of the difference.

Inevitably, some of these alternatives started to throw in their lot with consumer capitalism, 'demutualizing' to the short-term financial advantage of their current members. Money-spinning scams of the kind associated with predatory hucksters and executives chasing a quick buck wherever they could find it, began to encircle them. Seen from this perspective, the future of cooperative and mutual endeavor – and their legacy to fair trade – looks a little bleak.

But we should not be deceived. Those that remain are prospering from their political (often restyled 'ethical') appeal. To the same extent that the old mutual enterprises have thrown in the towel, unmet needs – even in rich countries – have reemerged in the deep structures of society, in the growing chasm between rich and poor. What's more, the vast majority of the world's people remains on the wrong side of the divide and are of only marginal interest to consumer capitalism. Though they must live under its shadow, they frequently work together with the mutuality that generalized human well-being invariably demands.

Real benefits

One doesn't have to be romantic about this, or glorify poverty in any way, to appreciate that fair trade has a res- onance well beyond the confines of any 'market niche'. Over the years I have seen dozens of fair-trade projects at work in the South, and in every single one of them the benefits were not in question, merely why there wasn't more of it and what could be done to make it bigger. Though fair trade may be an infant among giants, the future lies with the infant, not the giant.

If this is so, then its importance means that there are some serious questions fair trade will eventually have to answer about its credentials. How different is it really? Is fair trade merely out to inject 'ethical' con- siderations into a system that otherwise remains unchanged? Given all we know about world trade, wouldn't we be better off without it? At the very least, shouldn't we cut the 5,000 miles (8,000 kilometers) the average breakfast travels to our stomachs in the North, and 'go local' instead? More particularly, shouldn't the consumption of Southern food commodities in the North – fairly traded though they may be – be avoided when commodity trading is so inherently unstable and destructive?

Well, maybe. Of course, if the real environmental costs were paid, international trade would be very much more expensive – and less profitable. Of course, if vigorous labor movements achieved decent basic standards everywhere, there would be less incentive for transnational corporations to search out the best places for exploitation. Since it is at the local level that human relationships develop, this is where democratic control will eventually make a difference. Thinking globally and acting locally makes common sense.

However, even if all we want is to get from here to there, here is where we are. One might suggest to coffee farmers in Peru that it would have been better had they never colonized the Tambopata River Valley, displaced indigenous people or weakened the fragile topsoil. But this is where they are, and no amount of wishful thinking is going to put them anywhere else. While they are here, they depend entirely on the international coffee trade. Fair trade helps them to care for their environment and take more control over their own lives. When they have done so, and if others have done so too, then they'll be better placed to decide for themselves what next to do for the best.

Global and local

Besides, there is nothing inherently more just about 'the local'. Local chauvinism can be a very ugly thing indeed. Retreating through history to feudal Europe or Aztec Mexico scarcely takes us to a more appealing destination. Moving sideways to the surviving wisdom of indigenous peoples may be a valuable exercise, but it doesn't tell us where to place the next step.

The distinction that matters is between globalization and internationalism. Where the former imposes itself through the existing division of wealth and power, the latter advances the principle of democratic control, which of necessity enhances local diversity. Fair trade, properly understood, is an expression of this principle. That doesn't have to mean taking coffee off the breakfast table altogether.

Fair trade's promise

The promise is that fair trade's higher price goes straight to impoverished producers in the South. It is important that this promise is kept. However, fair trade differs from charity. A cast-iron consumer guarantee about exactly where the 'premium' goes – as if it were a charitable donation – would require a large bureaucracy to administer and take up most of the premium itself. It would doubtless also have to be run from the North and establish yet another dictatorship over producers – something fair trade has to be watchful to prevent.

What's more, fair-trade agreements often involve a minimum-price guarantee which only kicks in when world commodity prices fall below a certain level – usually the real cost of production. If, in a rare boom year, the price goes higher then the fair-trade producers' premium doesn't apply and the nature of the promise changes. In fact, fair trade faces its toughest test during boom years, when the need for it is no longer so obvious and *coyote* middlemen quickly reappear on the scene to make producers tempting short-term offers.

Fair trade is about long-term commitments that outlast the slumps and booms of conventional trade. Corporations make their profit from the monopolistic control they exercise over markets – over both consumers and producers. Their 'margins' come from the difference between the low price they pay producers and what they can charge consumers. Their position of power means they can force down the one and force up the other, regardless of the real or relative value of what's for sale.

While corporations may compete among themselves for consumers and 'market share', they all have a shared interest in keeping their 'costs of production' as low as possible and enhancing their margins. The more fair trade grows and takes control of these margins away from corporations, the more of the difference will remain with producers and consumers – and the need for the fair-trade premium will disappear. In any case and as we have seen, commodities are far too cheap and will have to become very much more expensive if anything is to be left of them at all. The transfer of wealth from poor to rich, South to North, that this represents is a scandal comparable in scale to that of debt, the full dimensions of which remain to be properly exposed.

Look at the label

Northern consumers can, and should, rely on fair-trade labeling in supermarkets. But experience of eco-labeling tells us how careful we have to be. A label is, of itself, quite worthless. It may be imbued with all the mystique of a 'brand' – the costs of which account for a sizable chunk of the price you pay – but for fair-traders it has another job to do, identifying people you are better able to trust because you know who they are. Where conventional trade hides behind a veil of commercial secrecy, fair trade makes a virtue of telling you more. You may not be able to change the world as much as you would like by shopping with your eyes open – but keeping them closed makes absolutely certain that it stays the same.

That is not really an option. Far from being bastions of liberty, corporations operate as their very own 'command economies' – more Stalinist than Stalin himself. In the export-processing factory I visited in Ciudad Juárez, Mexico – owned by the Dutch electronics giant Philips – every employee was required to sign a statement that read as follows: 'For some of us, the Company is very much like a Leader or a Big Brother watching over us; many fail to appreciate just how big and diverse it is.' Without any hint of irony, the document spelt out what is implicit in the way all corporations operate.

By way of an alternative, people have been making their own, flexible, international network of associations, trade unions and cooperatives, consumer and environmental organizations – a self-propelled 'swarm' that is finally beginning to have an impact on world events. Fair trade is, or will become, just one physical expression of these networks.

Campus campaign

Consider a small but significant sign of change. On university campuses in the US a largely unreported student movement against sweatshop labor – in the global South, Los Angeles or anywhere else – has been growing for some time. It has passed from one generation of students to the next, questioning the attitude of academic institutions towards increasingly pervasive corporate sponsorship.

Nowhere is this more pronounced than in sports, where the globalization of the equipment industry and of corporate brands is almost complete. College sports are the seedbed of this process in the US. Yet in May 2000 Nike, stung by persistent campus criticism of its employment practices, started to withdraw sponsorship from the sports teams of some of the more critical colleges. Designed no doubt as a threat, the corporation may equally well turn out to have been slitting its own throat.

The anti-sweatshop movement in the US grew and dug in its heels because it established links with real people and issues that are difficult to distort forever. In turn, it generated an interest in the wider world – like what the World Trade Organization was up to in

Seattle in November 1999. Here, for the first time, a generation of young Americans took issue with global capital and corporate America on the streets of an American city.

A similar process is underway around the world. The superficial signs are now visible wherever globalization surfaces, at gatherings of the WTO, IMF, World Bank and at G7/8 summits in particular. Despite the coverage given to high-profile 'riots' in the North, the extent of this resistance, particularly in the South, goes largely unreported by the Northern media. That does not mean that it does not exist. The corporate project, as it knows to its cost, now has to advance over vigorously contested ground whichever way it turns.

Two problems are now critical. The first is how to untie the knot that has so far held globalized labor down. On the face of it, President Clinton and the US Government were advancing its cause when they advocated at the time of the 1999 WTO meeting in Seattle that basic labor standards should form part of WTO agreements. This was resolutely resisted by some Southern governments, in a curious alliance with corporate interests, on the grounds that it was a cynical appeal to nationalist sentiments designed to protect US jobs and increase the electoral appeal of the Democrats – at the expense of the South.

Union struggle

Yet, if you talk to trade unionists engaged in the desperate struggle to gain ground in the South, it is precisely the basic standards of the International Labor Organization that they are now trying to secure. Perhaps there is a confusion here. What this means, more often than not, is the right to organize at all. There have been powerful objections to the entry of China to the WTO because of the absence of free trade unions in the communist legacy. Well, how about

The net works

With a bit of imagination, it's possible to foresee a world in which trade expresses rather than suppresses the relationship between people. **Michael Barratt Brown**, *whose work has been instrumental in the development of fair trade, sketches a few outlines of what this might look like.*

At the lowest level of the housing estate or village or block of flats, groups would form elected community councils. These would then have responsibility for certain services – cleaning, laundering, gardening, plumbing and minor building repairs – for which they could make a charge, and also for renting out premises for workshops and retail outlets, shops and restaurants, from which they would receive an income to use as they saw fit, to improve the environment, for recreation grounds, parks, crèches, etc. Through horizontal linkages they would network with similar estates and villages and blocks of flats in wards and districts, including the surrounding countryside, both to provide appropriate services in housing, health, education, garbage collection, footpaths, swimming pools, larger parks and playing fields, and so draw upon those enterprises producing for local needs – fruit and vegetables, bakeries, housing materials, repair shops, etc. Contracts and prices would then be the subject of negotiation on quality and service between representatives of the workers, the groups of households and the elected local authority at district level. The authorities would also need to obtain supplies from outside the district. This could be done by building links with enterprises whose products suited their needs. By adding here the element of networking, these links could be strengthened into firm and continuing relationships allowing for forward planning beyond a single purchase or contract. This happens now, where public purchasing officers have found suppliers that they can rely on to understand their special needs. District authorities could also help to finance specialized networks, such as ethnic minorities, who want to develop provision for their own particular needs and tastes. These could include many of the organizations that are now involved in alternative trade.

In this model the communities and districts form the real building blocks of decentralized power, with their own elected councils and much-extended responsibilities. For it is at this level that people can meet each other and get to know each other's interests, share common facilities and feel a common responsibility for the care and protection of the neighborhood.

District and community councils can do much to strengthen social provision for all. But in the provision of personal and household needs we shall also have to bring a higher level of power to bear, where large numbers can be deployed to make up for individual financial weakness. Cities and counties comprise populations of several million and it is to them that we must look for the necessary power to influence household provision so that the needs of the poorer households are catered for.

At the level of the city and the county we are not only dealing with a much larger population and with health, education, police, fire brigades and public transport appropriate to the scale, but there will be productive enterprises, factories, mines and quarries, refineries and the like which have a national as well as an international market. It would be reasonable to imagine loosely, vertically integrated competing networks being based on cities and counties. In this case the power of a city or county authority would be enough to ensure that suppliers inside the network catered equally for the full range of income groups. Regional differences in income and tastes could then be allowed for. If cities and counties build up their own networks of suppliers, there is no reason why they should not link with neighboring cities and counties to widen their network.

When we reach the level of the nation-state, the question arises of the relationship between, on the one hand, the networks and the enterprises to which they are linked, and on the other, the arrangements to be made for allocating resources. Setting the parameters should surely be the limit of central responsibility, whether this is exercised by a state or federal body. For clearing the payments of international trade we have to envisage a much wider international structure than a federation.

Within these general parameters of resource allocation, networks should be free to make their own linkages and compete for business. The networks could not be said to be effective, competing traders if they could not set their own prices and make their own investments. If there were a great plurality of these networks for households to belong to, and if they were self-financing, not only enjoying the income of grants and subscriptions but also of their networking activities, they would have as much power as the giant companies today – but they would be subject to the democratic control of their members.

There remains the question of the relationship of the producing enterprises and the networks to the universal international system of resource allocation. Some of the enterprises may be quite large, supplying several, or even many, networks. They will want to have direct relations with the allocating center. Even if this is not a nation-state it will need to have the capacity to set norms for the operation of enterprises and to see that they are observed.

The great remaining problem is the necessity of imagining an international regulator and allocator of resources that does not replicate the bureaucracies of nation-states and of existing federations of states. Given the plurality of networks which is envisaged here, effective international representation of these networks, or of groups of networks, would have to be provided for. The setting of parameters for the operation of both networks and enterprises seems likely to imply something more continuous than occasional rounds of negotiation. One solution to this problem would be a world economic parliament, based on networks, a second Chamber of Peoples to complement the United Nations General Assembly, which is based on geographical nation-state constituencies. ■

from Michael Barratt Brown, *Fair Trade*, Zed Books, London, 1993 their continuing repression in places like Guatemala because of the corporate legacy? What, precisely, is the difference? There's a special kind of idiocy in the suggestion – which free-traders frequently make – that trade has at once no relationship whatever with anything else in places like Guatemala, and a liberating political effect in places like China.

WTO in Seattle

The question in Seattle was less whether a 'social' clause should be attached to WTO agreements than whether the WTO, in its present form, can sensibly be given any more power than it already has – to which the answer was, of course, a resounding 'No'. But the labor issue cannot be dodged. There is absolutely no reason why the WTO in any form – or anyone else, for that matter – should have license to ignore the most basic of human rights as established in the UN's International Labor Organization (ILO) agreements and the Universal Declaration of Human Rights. Corporations and their allies are more than happy to pass the parcel to the ILO because they know it has no teeth. Trade has fangs.

The second problem concerns the environment. It surfaced at Seattle in the form of the European Union's position on some key issues – and genetically modified organisms in particular. The WTO dictates that if there are no scientific objections to it, trade must be unrestricted. The environmental implications of this are potentially catastrophic – any 'scientific' stamp of approval secured by corporations in the US, for example, could then be used to impose corporate interests across the world. More immediately, present WTO rules trump the far saner 'precautionary principle', whereby the burden of proof rests with safety rather than risk.

Trade-related environmental issues surface on supermarket shelves in the form of 'organic' alternatives. These have been given added prominence – and sometimes prices to match – by recent food scares in the North. Every fair-trade food project I have visited took an active interest in organic methods – in good measure, for sure, because of higher prices, but also (and increasingly) because of the devastating impact on their own health of chemical poisons. If this has not yet surfaced in the consumer consciousness of the North, it has not been for want of trying, though the fact that Southern producers usually die young and with little attention to the cause may have a good deal to do with it as well.

The eventual choice before us – when the poisons no longer work or have killed everything that moves – is likely to be between organic methods and genetic modification. In view of the terrifying implications of the latter, it's not altogether surprising that agribusiness presents it as 'inevitable'. But it's the structure of trade, rather than of genes, that is in need of modification. There is no earthly reason why organic production should not also be fairly traded – or why fairly traded production should not also be organic. The one cannot prosper without the other.

The arbiter of reason

The edifice of free trade rests on the notion that price is not merely the best, but the only, arbiter of reason. In a competitive free market you get what you pay for. Everything else is too vulnerable to 'distortion' and 'political interference' to be relied upon. But we've already seen that cheap commodities – and therefore low inflation in the North – result from overtly political interference in the South by the North through the mechanism of debt. The call to keep politics out of trade is pure humbug.

Besides, as huge corporations consume each other and merge into undifferentiated blobs, the myth of fierce international competition is becoming threadbare. Any competition tends to be between governments for the favor of corporations, or between impoverished people for a job, rather than between transnational corporations for a larger share of world markets they already monopolize. In such circumstances, the price of a thing tells us little more than what the prevailing disposition of wealth and power can get away with.

Consumer responsibility

Fair trade, on the other hand, recognizes the responsibility we have for the consequences of what we buy. This returns us to the question we asked about the perfect pair of blue jeans: if consumers pay less than the real cost, who pays the rest? Neither impoverished producers nor the environment will put up with exploitation forever. Sooner or later, in one way or another, consumer capitalism will have to pay its own bills. What's unique about fair trade is that it is not just a theoretical option but a practical alternative that's already in place.

It's now more or less routine to dismiss the UN, and the United Nations Conference on Trade and Development (UNCTAD) in particular, as hopelessly unequal to the task. I have personal reasons for thinking so. Quite by chance I was in Santiago, Chile, during the preparations for an UNCTAD conference in 1972. For a few weeks beforehand, quaint little machines ran around town painting fresh white lines on the city streets. An earthquake-proof conference center was built at great public expense to accommodate the conference delegates.

The only time we ever saw them was when tear gas aimed at demonstrators outside was accidentally sucked into the air-conditioning system and they came spluttering onto the streets. All the while, big US corporations like ITT (directly assisted by the US Government – oh yes, we have chapter and verse, now that it's too late) were busy dismantling the elected government of

Popular Unity and President Salvador Allende by strangling the country's trade. No-one at the UNCTAD conference in Santiago seemed unduly troubled by this, even though they were right in the middle of it. By contrast, when General Pinochet bombed the presidential palace, killed Salvador Allende and usurped power in 1973, he found the country's trading partners extremely obliging, and moved his seat of government into the UNCTAD conference center.

For all its failings, in recent years some of the sharpest rethinking on international trade has come out of UNCTAD. If it now decided to support fair trade with just a fraction of the backing given to unfair trade by the WTO, fair trade might flourish more vigorously than anyone currently suspects – or fears – is possible.

What prevents UNCTAD from getting cracking? Its members. Who are its members? Our governments. What prevents them from getting cracking? Either the inertia of those of us who employ them in countries with democratic pretensions, or the repression of those who live in countries without democracy.

Capitalism's weakness

Though the power of consumer capitalism is enormous, it has shallow roots and is therefore neither invulnerable nor quite so pervasive as it would have us believe. Its view is myopic, not of the world as it is but of the way it would like it to be. You don't have to travel very far from the citadels of corporate power to notice the difference. In this respect, consumer capitalism is no more – and perhaps considerably less – realistic in its outlook than those of us who see the world very differently.

The promise of free trade is that it will deliver the goods in the end. But there comes a point when a promise is exposed as fake. Perhaps that point has now been reached, so that before too long we'll be looking back and wondering what kept us waiting.

Labeling

Many fairly traded products are now on superstore shelves – if they are not, keep asking why not. An effective system of labeling is essential to inform consumers, fend off fakers and encourage the rest. Look for their labels wherever you are.

The Fair Trade Labeling Organizations International (FLO) is the umbrella body for all the major fair-trade labels and can be contacted at:

Kaiser-Friedrich Strasse 13, D-53113 Bonn, Germany
Tel: +49 228 949230, Fax: +49 228 2421713
E-mail: coordination@fairtrade.net   Website: www.fairtrade.net

Its members include the following:

Austria: TransFair Austria, Wipplingerstr. 32, A-1010 Wien.
Tel: +43 1 53309561, Fax: +43 1 5330957, E-mail: transfair.a@magnet.at
Website: www.oneworld.at/transfair/
Belgium: Max Havelaar Belgie, Boulevard Leopold II, 184 D, B-1080
Brussels. Tel: +32 2 411 64 62, Fax: +32 2 411 60 05,
E-mail: info@maxhavelaar.be
Britain: Fairtrade Foundation, Suite 204, 16 Baldwins Gardens, London
EC1N 7RJ. Tel: +44 20 7 4055942, Fax: +44 2 07 4055943,
E-mail: mail@fairtrade.org.uk   Website: www.gn.apc.org/fairtrade/
Canada (Associate member)**:** Transfair Canada / Fair TradeMark, 8323
Chapel Street, 2nd floor, Ottawa, Ontario K1N 7Z2. Tel: +1 613 5633351,
Fax: +1 613 2375969, E-mail: fairtrade@cyberus.ca
Website: www.web.net/fairtrade
Denmark: c/o FKN, Nørregade 13 kld, DK-1165, Københaven K.
Tel: +45 33 11 1345, Fax: +45 33 11 1347. E-mail: info@maxhavelaar.dk
Website: www.maxhavelaar.dk
Finland (Associate member)**:** Reilun kaupan edistämisyhdistys ry,
Ludviginkatu 3-5 B42, O0130 Helsinki. Tel: +358 9 643153,
Fax: +358 9 643156, E-mail: reilukey@kaapeli.fi   Website: www.kepa.fi/merkki
France: Max Havelaar France, 41 Rue Emile Zola, F-93100 Montreuil.
Tel: +33 1 42877021, Fax: +33 1 48700768, E-mail: Mhavelaar@aol.com
Germany: TransFair Germany, Remigiusstr. 21, 50937 Köln.
Tel: +49 221 9420400, Fax: +49 221 9420404; E-mail: info@transfair.org
Website: www.transfair.org
Ireland: Fairtrade Mark Ireland, PO Box 6031, Dublin 6. Tel: +353 1 475 3515,
Fax: 353 1 475 3515, E-mail: fair.mark@pobox.com
Italy: Transfair Italy, Piazzetta Forzate 1, 1-35137 Padova.
Tel: +39 049 8750 823, Fax: +39 049 8750 910, E-mail: transfai@intercity.it
www.citinv.it/equo/homefair.htm
Japan (Associate member)**:** Transfair Japan, c/o St Paul Lutheran Church
of the JELC, 5-3-1 Koutoubashi, Sumida-ku, Tokyo 130.
Tel: +81 3 36347867, Fax: +81 3 36347808, E-mail wakatiai@mail.big.or.jp
Luxembourg: Transfair Minka Luxembourg, 13 Rue de la Gare, L-5353
Oetrange. Tel: +352 350762, Fax: 352 350762, E-mail: transfair@pt.lu
Netherlands: Stichting Max Havelaar, Postbus 1252, NL-3512 BG,
Utrecht. Tel: +31 3- 2334602, Fax: +31 30 2332992,
E-mail: maxhavelaar@maxhavelaar.nl   Website: www.maxhavelaar.nl

Norway: Max Havelaar, Storgata 11, 0155 Oslo. Tel: +47 23 010330,
Fax: +47 23 010331, E-mail: maxhavelaar@maxhavelaar.no
Website: www.maxhavelaar.no
Sweden: Föreningen för Rättvisemärkt, Drakenbergsgatan 11, SE-117 41
Stockholm. Tel: +46 8 668 0350, Fax: +46 8 668 0314,
E-mail: handla@raettvist.se   Website: www.raettvist.se
Switzerland: Max Havelaar Stiftung Schweiz, Malzgasse 25, CH-4052
Basel. Tel: +41 61 271500, Fax: +41 61 271562,
E-mail: postmaster@maxhavelaar.ch
USA (Associate member)**:** Transfair USA, 52 Ninth Street, Oakland CA
94607. Tel: +1 510 6635260, Fax: +1 510 6635264,
E-mail: transfair@transfairusa.org

Trading

**There's an enormous range of fair-trade products available
from alternative outlets. Here the label matters less than
the organization – whether it's an aid agency or an alternative trading organization (ATO).**

The International Federation for Alternative Trade (IFAT) is a global network
of 143 fair-trade organizations in 47 countries, many of them Southern producers, and can be contacted at:

**30 Murdock Road, Bicester, Oxon OX6 7RF, UK
Tel: +44 1869 249 819, Fax: +44 1869 246 381
E-mail: cwills@ifat.org.uk Website: www.ifat.org**

Here are just a few of its members – they can put you in touch with their
partners in the South:

Aotearoa/New Zealand: Trade Aid Importers Ltd, 174 Gayhurst Road,
PO Box 35-049, Christchurch. Tel: +64 3 385 3535, Fax: +64 3 385 3536,
E-mail: stephena@tradeaid.co.nz Website: www.tradeaid.co.nz
Australia: Community Aid Abroad Trading, 278 Grand Junction Road,
Athol Park, SA 5012. Tel: +61 1800 088 455 (toll free from within Australia)
or +61 8 83410555, E-mail: mailord@caatrading.org.au
Website: www.caatrading.org.au
Britain: Oxfam Fair Trade Co, 274 Banbury Road, Oxford OX2 7DZ.
Tel: +44 1865 311311, Fax: +44 1865 313163,
E-mail: astevens@oxfam.org.uk Website: www.oxfam.org.uk

Traidcraft Exchange, Kingsway, Gateshead, Tyne & Wear, NE11 0NE.
Tel: +44 191 491 0591, Fax: +44 191 482 2690,
E-mail: alanb@traidcraft.co.uk   Website: www.globalnet.co.uk/-traidcraft

Equal Exchange Trading Limited, 10A Queensferry Street, Edinburgh EH2
4DF. Tel: +44 131 220 3484, Fax: +44 131 220 3565,
E-mail: campaign@gn.apc.org

Twin Trading, 3rd Floor, 1 Curtain Road, London EC2A 3CT. Tel: +44 20
7375 1221, Fax: +44 20 7375 1337,
E-mail: info@twin.org.uk
Canada: Ten Thousand Villages (Canada), PO Box 869, New Hamburg,
Ontario, N0B 2G0. Tel: +1 519 662 1879, Fax: +1 519 662 3755,
E-mail: doug@villages.ca Website: www.tenthousandvillages.com

Contacts

Central America: (Trade Union) UNSITRAGUA, 9a Avenida 1-43, Zona 1, Guatemala City, Guatemala, Central America, Tel/Fax: +502 238 2272, E-mail: unsitragua@pronet.net.gt
Ireland: Irish Fair Trade Network, Little Orchard, Newpark, Kilkenny. Tel: +353 56 63733, Fax: +353 56 63220, E-mail: cbergin@connect.ie
Japan: Global Village Fair Trade Company, Noge 1-13-16, Setagaya-ku, Tokyo 158. Tel: +81 33 705 0233, Fax: +81 33 705 0255, E-mail: gv@gn.apc.org Website: www.globalvillage.or.jp
South Africa: Just Exchange, PO Box 13154, Mowbray, Cape Town 7705. Tel: +27 21 448 6672, Fax: +27 21 473 498, E-mail: justex@wn.apc.org Website: www.peoplink.org/just-exchange
USA: Equal Exchange, 251 Revere Street, Canton, MA 02021. Tel: +1 781 830 0303, Fax: +1 781 830 0282, E-mail: jrosenthal@equalexchange.com Website: www.equalexchange.com

Ten Thousand Villages (USA), 704 Main Street, PO Box 5000, Akron, Pa. 17501-0500. Tel: +1 717 8598100, Fax: 1 717 859 2622, Website: www.villages.ca

Bibliography

Fair Trade by Michael Barratt Brown (Zed Books, London and New Jersey, 1993). Barratt Brown has been a pivotal figure not just in thinking through the ideas but in putting them into practice.

The Canadian journalist Naomi Klein has come up with *No Logo* (Flamingo, London, 2000). This is a snappy tour round some of the brand-name issues. She concludes that improving labor conditions is a more relevant issue – and fair trade runs the risk of sanitizing the system.

No Sweat: Fashion, Free Trade and the Rights of Garment Workers edited by Andrew Ross (Verso, New York and London, 1997), an anthology of features and pictures that give you a rare glimpse into the abyss beneath the fashion business.

A closer look at related development issues can be found in John Madeley's *Trade and the Poor – The impact of international trade on developing countries* (Intermediate Technology Publications, London, 1996).

A surprisingly productive mine of information hides beneath the UN Conference on Trade and Development (UNCTAD). You can write for information direct to their Sales Section in New York or Geneva or visit their website (www.unctad.org). While most of their statistics and reports are for trade junkies only, the pages of their annual *Trade and Development Report* have recently begun to include some of the most lucid analysis available anywhere.

The editions of the *New Internationalist* used in the text are as follows:
Trade Wars, no. 204, February 1989
Coffee – Spilling the Beans, no. 271, September 1995
The Big Jeans Stitch-up, no. 302, June 1998
The Cocoa Chain, no. 304, August 1998
The Big Banana Split, no. 317, October 1999
Fair Trade, no. 322, April 2000

www.newint.org

Index

Index

Index